A CACHE OF
Clevernesses

ANTONY LAKE

HART PUBLISHING COMPANY, INC.
NEW YORK CITY

COPYRIGHT © 1974

HART PUBLISHING COMPANY, INC., NEW YORK, N.Y. 10012
ISBN NO. 08055-0165-7
LIBRARY OF CONGRESS CATALOG CARD NO. 73-90271

NO PART OF THIS BOOK MAY BE REPRODUCED OR USED
IN ANY FORM WITHOUT THE EXPRESS PERMISSION OF
THE PUBLISHER IN WRITING.

MANUFACTURED IN THE UNITED STATES OF AMERICA

CONTENTS

PROBLEMS *Continued*

CLASSIC STANZAS

These verses are all well known, either for their brevity or their wit, which in some cases amount to the same thing.

ODE ON THE ANTIQUITY OF FLEAS

Adam
Had 'em!

❋

ONTOLOGICAL REFLECTION ON THE MEANING OF EXISTENCE

I—
Why?

❋

ODE ON THE CONDITION OF THE UNITED STATES AFTER SEVERAL YEARS OF PROHIBITION

Wet
Yet.

❋

Sir, I admit your general rule,
That every poet is a fool:
But you yourself may serve to show it,
That every fool is not a poet.

Matthew Prior

❋

ODE TO THE BRAHMINS OF BOSTON

Here's to dear old Boston,
  The home of the bean and the cod;
Where the Lowells speak only to Cabots,
  And the Cabots speak only to God.

COLOGNE

In Köln, a town of monks and bones,
And pavements fanged with murderous stones,
And rags, and hags, and hideous wenches,
I counted two-and-seventy stenches,
All well defined, and separate stinks!
Ye nymphs that reign o'er sewers and sinks,
The river Rhine, it is well known,
Doth wash your city of Cologne;
But tell me, nymphs, what power divine
Shall henceforth wash the river Rhine?

Samuel Taylor Coleridge

※

Lives of great men oft remind us
    As we o'er their pages turn
That we, too, may leave behind us
    Letters that we ought to burn.

Thomas Hood

※

I do not love thee, Doctor Fell,
The reason why I cannot tell,
But this one thing I know full well:
I do not love thee, Doctor Fell.

Thomas Brown

※

A Christian is a man who feels
    Repentance on a Sunday
For what he did on Saturday
    And is going to do on Monday.

Thomas Russell Ybarra

Sir Christopher Wren
Said, "I am going to dine with some men.
If anybody calls
Say I am designing St. Paul's."

❀

OH, TO BE IN ENGLAND NOW THE WEATHER'S THERE!

Ah, lovely Devon . . .
Where it rains eight days out of seven!

❀

O what a tangled web we weave
When first we practice to deceive!
But when we've practiced quite a while
How vastly we improve our style!

J. R. Pope

❀

Great fleas have little fleas upon their back to bite 'em;
And little fleas have lesser fleas, and so *ad infinitum.*

❀

Seven wealthy towns contend for Homer dead;
Through which the living Homer had to beg his bread.

CRACKS FROM THE CRITICS

DOROTHY PARKER

The House Beautiful is the play lousy.

※

ROBERT GARLAND

This show has to be seen to be depreciated.

※

MONTY WOOLLEY

For the first time in my life I envied my feet. They were asleep.

※

JOHN ANDERSON

The audience was so quiet, you could hear a pun drop.

※

IRVING HOFFMAN

This show goes on my Best Smeller list.

※

PERCY HAMMOND

I have knocked everything but the chorus girls' legs, and here God anticipated me.

FRANK NUGENT

A run of DeMille picture—March comes in like a lion and goes out like a ham.

⚜

EUGENE FIELD

The actor who took the role of *King Lear* played the king as though he expected someone to play the ace.

⚜

GROUCHO MARX

I saw the show under bad conditions—the curtain was up.

⚜

J. NORMAN LYND

The quartet sang a derangement of an old favorite.

⚜

ROBERT BENCHLEY

Perfectly Scandalous was one of those plays in which all of the actors unfortunately enunciated very clearly.

⚜

ALEXANDER WOOLLCOTT

The scenery was beautiful—but the actors got in front of it.

BROOKS ATKINSON

When Mr. Wilbur calls his play *Halfway to Hell*, he underestimates the distance.

※

ANONYMOUS

Last night the High School band played Beethoven. Beethoven lost.

※

I just saw Isherwood's play *I Am a Camera*.
No Leica.

LETTER-PERFECT

It's really not that tough to construct a sentence which employs every letter of the alphabet at least once. The trick comes in when you try to keep the *total* number of letters in the sentence down to a bare minimum. A letter-perfect sentence of this sort would, naturally, employ 26 letters—no more, no less. Take a look at these near misses.

A QUICK BROWN FOX JUMPS OVER THE LAZY DOG.
(33 letters)

PACK MY BOX WITH FIVE DOZEN LIQUOR JUGS.
(32 letters)

QUICK WAFTING ZEPHYRS VEX·BOLD JIM.
(29 letters)

And here's the best one we've ever seen, employing only 28 letters. (If you come up with a more economical sentence of this kind, let us know *immediately.*)

WALTZ, NYMPH, FOR QUICK JIGS VEX BUD.

ALLITERATIVE RHYMES

Here is a selection of *tours de force* concocted by some of our wilier versifiers.

Cardinal Wolsey was the son of a butcher. With his rapid rise to political eminence, he managed to draw an unhealthy quota of jealous antagonists. William Pitt made capital of Wolsey's humble origin by lampooning him in these lines:

> *Begot by butchers, but by butchers bred,*
> *How high His Highness holds his haughty head.*

A couple of centuries ago, the medical profession was not held in high repute—perhaps with good cause. Here are some anonymous lines that reflect the temper of the day:

> *Medical men my mood mistaking,*
> *Most mawkish, monstrous messes making,*
> *Molest me much.*
> *More manfully my mind might meet my malady.*
> *Medicine's mere mockery murders me.*

Addressed to the same group, here are some playful lines:

> *I need not your needles,*
> *They're needless to me;*
> *For kneading of needles*
> *Were needless you see.*

> *But did my neat trousers*
> *But need to be kneed—*
> *I then should have need*
> *Of your needles, indeed!*

David Garrick, likely the most famous English actor of the 18th century, patronized an apothecary and physician by the name of Dr. John Hill. When Hill died, Garrick penned his obituary in the following lines:

> *For physic and farces*
> *His equal there scarce is;*
> *His farces are physic,*
> *His physic a farce is!*

But it took one Mr. Poulter, a resident of Winchester, England, to top all previous efforts. He composed what is probably the longest alliterative poem on record. Poulter ran the full gamut from A to Z, as witness the following:

> *An Austrian army, awfully arrayed,*
> *Boldly by battery, besieged Belgrade.*
> *Cossack commanders cannonading come*
> *Dealing destruction's devastating doom.*
> *Every endeavor engineers essay*
> *For fame, for fortune, forming furious fray.*
> *Gaunt gunners grapple, giving gashes good,*
> *Heaves high his head, heroic hardihood.*
> *Ibraham, Islam, imps in ill,*
> *Jostle John Jarovlitz, Jem, Joe, Jack, Jill;*
> *Kick kindling Kutosoff, king's kinsmen kill.*
> *Labor low levels loftiest, longest lines.*
> *Men march mid moles, mid mounds, mid murd'rous mines,*
> *Now nightfall's near; now needful nature nods,*
> *Opposed, opposing, overcoming odds,*
> *Poor peasants, partly purchased, partly pressed,*
> *Quite quaking, quarter, quarter quickly quest.*
> *Reason returns, recalls redundant rage,*
> *Saves sinking soldiers, softens Signiors sage.*
> *Truce, Turkey, truce, treacherous Tartar train,*
> *Unwise, unjust unmerciful Ukraine,*
> *Vanish vile vengeance, vanish victory vain.*
> *Wisdom wails war, wails warring words.*
> *Xerxes, Xanthippus, Ximines, Xavier,*
> *Yet Yassey's youth ye yield your youthful yest,*
> *Zealously, zanes, zealously, zeals zest.*

APPROPRIATE ADVERBS

"I wish I'd made that bet," said the bookmaker, hoarsely.

※

"I must attend to my flock," said the vicar, sheepishly.

※

"Bing Crosby might get a sore throat," said Bob, hopefully.

※

"But I don't want a spaniel, I want a corgi," said the pet-fancier, doggedly.

※

"Do you think you understand my painting?" asked Picasso, artfully.

※

"Your drip-dries are crumpled," said the laundress, ironically.

※

"I only want 20,000 machine guns," said the dictator, disarmingly.

※

"This is an imitation diamond," said the dealer, stonily.

※

"I practiced three hours on my guitar," said the folk singer, pluckily.

※

"Dear Sirs, please send me your catalogue," he wrote, listlessly.

※

"These pants are not short enough," said the young girl, hotly.

"May I leave the room?" asked the schoolboy, high-handedly.

🌿

"What an ample bosom!" he remarked, robustly.

🌿

"My Chinese necklace has been stolen," she said, jadedly.

🌿

"How do you like my petticoat?" she asked, shiftlessly.

🌿

"I am on the wrong street," said the Frenchman, ruefully.

🌿

"I have flunked this lousy exam," said the student, testily.

🌿

"My aim is true," said the swordsman, pointedly, as he lunged
toward his opponent.

🌿

"Have you anything by Hugo?" asked Les, miserably.

🌿

"I've $400.00, any more?" asked the auctioneer, morbidly.

🌿

"I don't *have* to do this for a living," she said, tartly.

🌿

"This river is rough," he said, rapidly.

🌿

"I wasn't there," she remarked, absently.

"My pencil is dull," he remarked, pointlessly.

※

"Press your own shirt!" she declared, flatly.

※

"I'll drive the truck," he whispered, shiftily.

※

"I've got all the work I can handle," the doctor said, patiently.

※

"I wish I could remember the name of that card game," she said, wistfully.

※

"I know everything about geometry," he remarked, plainly.

※

"I'll cut him to ribbons!" she scowled, mincingly.

※

"I slept in a draft last night," he remarked, stiffly.

※

"I can't stand strawberries," she said, rashly.

※

"May he rest in peace," the minister intoned, gravely.

※

"Yes, I've read *Gulliver's Travels*," he replied, swiftly.

※

"I tore his valentine in two," she said, halfheartedly.

"I work as a ditch-digger," he announced, trenchantly.

*

"We're out of pumpernickel," the baker said, wryly.

*

"Have you ever read Voltaire?" the teacher asked, candidly.

*

"My dime rolled into the sewer," the boy cried, gratefully.

*

"A mule is half donkey and half horse," he explained, crossly.

*

"You still haven't learned how to bake," her husband sneered, crustily.

*

"I hate shellfish!" she snapped, crabbedly.

*

"My glands are swollen," she said, mumpishly.

*

"My dog is terribly ill," the boy shouted, rabidly.

*

"This ain't real turtle soup!" the woman said, mockingly.

*

"He resembles a goat!" he chortled, satirically.

THE PROBLEM OF THE NOBLES
AND THE SLAVES

There is a certain tribe in Africa which knows not the meaning of mediocrity. There each person is either prince or pauper, benign or bad. A strict caste system sharply divides each of these groups into nobles and slaves. The standing of each caste is reflected in the integrity of its members: the nobles always tell the truth; the slaves are congenital liars.

An explorer who passed through this strange country had heard about the strange population. His first sight of its people was an encounter with three natives whom he espied on the other side of a rushing torrent.

The explorer, knowing the native tongue, shouted across the stream to the first man: "Are you a noble or are you a slave?" The native hastened to reply but his answer was lost in the sound of the rushing waters.

The second native had heard the question and seeing that the explorer did not grasp the first man's answer, he cried out: "This man says he's a noble. He *is* a noble. So am I a noble."

Whereupon the third native mockingly affirmed, pointing to the last speaker, "Put no trust in him! He's a slave; but I, I am a noble!"

Now the question is: Which of the three natives were nobles, and which of the three natives were slaves?

Answer on page 147

THE PROBLEM OF THE TELEPHONE CALL

A charming fellow, whom we'll call Winston, came home one evening at about 2 A.M., rather tired after the revels of the night. He went to bed directly. About twenty minutes later, he got up, opened the local telephone book, and looked up the number of one Gerald Malcolm. He called, and a sweet soprano answered.

"Hello! Is this Mrs. Malcolm?" queried Winston.

"Yes."

"I would like to speak to Mr. Malcolm."

"He's asleep."

"But it's very important!" Winston insisted.

"Important! Well, hold the wire a moment and I'll awaken him."

Young Winston glued his ear to the receiver long enough to hear Mrs. Malcolm walking off spouseward. *Then he deliberately hung up!!*

Now ruling out any hoax or wager, and hypothecating that Winston had never previously met or communicated with either Mr. or Mrs. Malcolm, and assuming that Winston acted premeditatedly and planned *everything* he did, what motive can you assign for his unparalleled action?

Answer on page 147

THE PROBLEM OF THE MOAT

Father takes little Oswald to the Zoo. Ozzie is especially attracted by the fierce alligators who lie exposed in the shallow water of a circular moat.

We now interrupt this story with some simple figures: The moat is six feet deep. In the center of it, there is a concrete island, which is exactly 11 feet away from the outer edge of the moat.

Little Ozzie gets sort of bumptious and flings his teddy-bear onto the island. He cries his head off, so his Pa decides to do something about the situation.

After scurrying around a while, Father finds two 10-foot planks but nothing to nail or bind them together. However, with the aid of those two pieces of wood, he somehow contrives to retrieve the teddy-bear—11 feet away. How does he do it?

Answer on page 147

THE PROBLEM OF THE DEAD TOURIST

Mr. and Mrs. Samuel Elkins, wealthy, sporting, society folks, went on a trip to Switzerland to enjoy some mountain climbing.

A few weeks later, the attractive Mrs. Elkins, shrouded in heavy black, returned to her home in Boston, a widow. Mr. Elkins had missed his step while on a climbing expedition, and had been precipitated headlong down a glassy ravine to a horrible death at the base of the mountain. It was a terrible accident and a terrible ordeal for the stricken Mrs. Elkins, who had been with him at the time and witnessed the tragedy.

About a month after Mrs. Elkins' return, her friends, who had given her their deepest sympathy, were astounded to hear that she had been indicted for the murder of her husband. But they were more shocked when Mrs. Elkins broke down and confessed!

The police had received the tip-off from a certain Mr. Harper, head of a well-known travel agency. Mr. Harper had never left the United States.

How did he deduce that Mrs. Elkins had murdered her husband?

Answer on page 147

THE PROBLEM OF THE STYMIED SAVAGE

A hapless missionary was captured by some wild aborigines. Having been condemned to death, the only question that remained was the manner of his dying.

According to tribal custom, this was to be decided by the voodoo man. Victims were told to make an affirmative statement. If the high priest considered the statement true, the victim would be shot with a poisoned arrow. If the statement was judged to be false, the victim would die a torturous death by fire. In any event, death apparently was a certainty—that is, to everyone except the crafty missionary.

He made a short statement which threw the voodoo man into such perplexity that it was found impossible to carry out the execution.

What words could that wily missionary have uttered?

Answer on page 147

THE PROBLEM OF THE PROFESSIONS

It is the last day of the 1974 Convention of the She Delta Deck Fraternity held at St. Louis. The Convention has been in session for a full week. Friends and acquaintances mingle in the lounge, smoking and chatting. Six of the members of the fraternity, peculiarly enough, bear the names of certain professions or trades. It is these six men with which this particular problem is concerned. Significant bits of their conversation are here recorded.

Mr. Grocer has been asked by Mr. Butcher to join him during the week in a round of golf. Mr. Grocer regrets he cannot accept.

Mr. Butcher replies, "How silly of me! You couldn't play golf now, anyhow. You told me you mashed your finger at your store under a tub of butter. Let me see it."

Mr. Doctor and Mr. Artist render the following colloquy:

Mr. Doctor: I go deep-sea fishing with the lawyer each week-end.

Mr. Artist: The doctor, the grocer, and I live in Milwaukee.

Mr. Baker has buttonholed Mr. Lawyer.

Mr. Baker: I got in a new and interesting case at the office. I'll drop in and tell you about it some time next week.

PROBLEM: Assume that none of these six men bears the name of his business or profession and assume that no two of these men are in the same business or profession, and further assume that one is a lawyer, one is a grocer, one is a doctor, one is an artist, one is a baker, and one is a butcher—

WHO IS THE LAWYER?   WHO IS THE BAKER?
WHO IS THE GROCER?   WHO IS THE BUTCHER?
WHO IS THE ARTIST?   WHO IS THE DOCTOR?

Answer on page 148

THE PROBLEM OF THE TWO STUDENTS

Two young boys appeared at the registrar's office at college. The clerk handed them questionnaires. Each boy subscribed to the following facts:

Each was named Jones. Each was born on February 3, 1957. Each was born at 120 East 57th Street, New York City. Each had a father named Joseph Jones. Each had a mother named Lillian Jones. After completing the questionnaires, the boys handed them to the registrar.

He read them and asked, "Are you two brothers?"

They replied, "Yes, we are." Glancing up from his papers, the registrar looked at the students. He noticed that they looked exactly alike and said, "You're twins, aren't you?"

Promptly they both answered, "No."

Assuming that all the answers they gave, both written and spoken, were accurate, and that they were both born of the same mother and father, how do you account for the fact that they were not twins?

Answer on page 149

THE PROBLEM OF THE TIRES

Charles Wayne Looksee, noted African explorer, is preparing to fulfill his life's ambition—to chart the trackless sands of the Sahara. A trip straight across the desert would be hazardous enough, but Looksee's journey will be doubly dangerous, since he must travel a roundabout route so as to make observations.

One of Looksee's biggest problems is equipment. For the automobile, he buys special heat-resistant tires, each of which is guaranteed to last 12,000 miles. It is extremely important that he does not load his car with any more weight than is necessary, so he determines to rely completely on the guarantee. Now the problem is: what is the least number of tires the explorer must buy to carry him through the 27,000-mile journey? And why?

Answer on page 149

THE PROBLEM OF THE MARKED FOREHEADS

A professor, wishing to determine who was the brightest among three of his cleverest students, named Alex, Joe, and Tom, arranged a little experiment. He had the three of them sit around a small circular table, each one facing the other two. Explaining that he was going to paste a little label on the forehead of each, he bade his three boys close their eyes. He told them that the labels would either be marked with a blue cross or a green cross. The challenge, he continued, consisted merely of this: that if any one of the students saw a green cross he should raise his hand, and that as soon as a student knew what color cross his forehead was marked with he should fold his arms on his breast.

While their eyes were shut, the professor proceeded to label each with a *green cross*. He then told the boys that all was set. They opened their eyes and each immediately raised his hand. After a lapse of a few minutes Alex folded his arms. The professor asked him how he was marked. Alex answered "Green." Can you explain the reasoning by which he made his deduction?

Answer on page 149

THE PROBLEM OF THE DIFFICULT CROSSING

A farmer must transport his dog, duck, and a bag of corn from one side of a river to the opposite bank. The craft he is using is very small—only large enough for him to take one of his possessions at any one time. If he leaves the dog alone with the duck, the dog is likely to make short work of the duck. If he leaves the duck alone with the corn, the duck will make short work of the corn.

What is the least number of trips the farmer can take to manage safely?

Answer on page 150

THE PROBLEM OF THE FRUIT PEDDLERS

Three fruit peddlers stood beside their pushcarts hawking their wares. They were each selling apples and each pushcart carried on it an identical price sign. The signs were the kind which are generally used by fruit peddlers in every market-place in the land.

The first peddler had fifteen apples to sell; he sold them all.

The second peddler had fourteen apples to sell; he sold them all.

The third peddler had thirteen apples to sell; he sold them all.

At the end of the day, they found that each had realized exactly the same amount of money for his apples.

The apples were *not* sold by weight or by measure. None of the apples was rotten; none of the apples was given away; none of the peddlers ate any of his apples, nor was any peddler given counterfeit money.

How do you account for the strange result?

Answer on page 150

THE PROBLEM OF THE MURDERED WOMAN

Serena Vashti Malloy, a rich dowager, was found murdered in her home in Chicago with a bullet through her heart. The local police ascertained that the murder was committed between 10 and 12 o'clock at night, and that the motive was robbery. They were also sure that the crime was committed by one of a notorious gang of local criminals.

They rounded up the gang, and at the preliminary arraignment each of the suspects was questioned. Each of the men made two significant statements. In each case, one of the statements was true, and one of the statements was false. (The order of the statements as presented is not controlling.)

The judge, aware of this state of affairs, deliberated awhile and soon became rightfully convinced of the guilt of one of the men in particular. Which one did he accuse?

The statements follow:

Mike: Red didn't kill her. I never saw a gun in my life.

Dan: I was in Philly when it happened. Matt did it.

Jim: Mike pulled the trigger. All of us except Dan were in Chi when it happened.

Spud: Only one of us witnessed the murder. I was not even in town on the night of the killing.

Matt: Spud's the murderer. I was at the neighborhood movies, at the time, with some other one of the boys.

Red: Me and Mike were together from 10 to 12 away from the rest of the gang. Dan killed her.

Answer on page 150

THE PROBLEM OF THE COMMUTER

Mr. Thaddeus Brown, a commuter, takes the same train every day, and arrives at his home station exactly at 5 P.M. He is met by his chauffeur the moment he steps off the train and is driven home. For the purposes of the problem, assume that no time is lost by Mr. Brown in getting into his automobile, nor that any time is consumed by the car in making the turn from the station toward the Brown estate.

One spring day, Brown leaves his office early and gets in at the station at exactly 4 P.M. His chauffeur, of course, has not arrived, and Brown, eager for exercise, starts to walk home. Later, en route, he is met by his car, on its way to the station to call for him. He gets in and is driven home to find that he has arrived at his residence 20 minutes earlier than usual.

Again assume that no time has been consumed by Brown's getting into the car and that the car, as usual, has made the turn in an inconsequential lapse of time. Now, hypothesizing that the car always travels at a uniform speed, how much time did Brown spend walking until he met his car?

Answer on page 152

THE PROBLEM OF THE JUGGLING JUGS

Two merchants in partnership have purchased an eight-quart jug of olive oil. They want to divide the oil into two equal parts. However, all they have on hand for purposes of measuring are two jugs—one of which holds five quarts, and the other three quarts.

At first it seems impossible to effect an even division of four quarts each by using the three containers on hand; but they finally manage to do it. Can you?

Answer on page 152

THE PROBLEM OF THE VANISHED COIN

The eight members of the Collector's Club were each considered experts and connoisseurs of objets d'art, stamps and coins. The Club did not admit outsiders to its meetings, and even insisted that the attendants not come in to replenish the bowls of fruit which invariably graced the long table at which the informal, fortnightly discussions were held.

One day one of the members met an acquaintance who was a numismatist. The friend had heard much about the famed discussions at the Collector's Club. He begged to be taken to that afternoon's meeting. Succumbing to his friend's entreaties, the member obtained permission to have him attend.

During the meeting, Mr. Grant Lewis, a coin collector just returned from a continental tour, exhibited his prize find. It was an ancient, rare Phoenician coin. The coin passed from hand to hand and was closely scrutinized by all those present. A continual barrage of questions was directed at the proud Lewis. Lewis was urged to expatiate on the history of his rare find. He requested the silver piece in order to point out certain peculiarities; but no one had the coin.

Each averred he had passed it to another, so that from the maze of statements it was impossible to determine who actually had the coin last. Every inch of the carpet was examined, but the coin seemed to have vanished into thin air. The members were upset. Someone asked who was playing the hoax, but the remark fell flat. Such a notion didn't square with the realization that the coin was worth a fabulous sum.

Finally, the demand was made that everyone submit to a personal examination. The suggestion was taken up and seconded with willingness by all—that is, *all except the stranger*. He demurred resolutely. Not only would he not submit to an examination, but he steadfastly refused to divulge any reason for his apparently stubborn refusal.

The chairman threatened to inform the police. As the dire words fell from the chairman's lips, Grant Lewis reached forth nervously into the silver bowl for an apple. As he drew the fruit away, there, at the bottom of the bowl, he saw his prize coin. Apologies poured forth upon the stranger, who rose to explain.

Now the explanation for his apparent obstinacy in refusing to be examined and refusing further to give a reason for his attitude was sound. All the facts necessary for a logical explanation of the stranger's actions are in the foregoing recital. What sensible and logical explanation did the stranger offer?

Answer on page 152

THE PROBLEM OF THE WHIFFLEBIRD

In the land of Nowhere, on a beautiful little hill, there once stood a small luxurious tree whose leaves were as sweet as nectar. To this tree there flew one day a Whifflebird. Tired from a long journey to the setting sun, he lighted on one branch of the tree and pecked at one of its leaves to refresh himself. It was delicious beyond compare, and he decided to remain there forever.

The next day he ate double the number of leaves he had eaten the first day. The third day, he ate double the number of leaves he had eaten the second day. And so on for thirty days till all the leaves were gone, and the beautiful little hill was crowned with a bare thorny stump. The Whifflebird did not tally his depredations, but you are asked to tell on what day half the foliage was gone.

Answer on page 153

THE PROBLEM OF THE CAT IN THE WELL

Through some misadventure, a cat fell down a well. The well was 18 feet deep. The cat managed to climb out, but only after experiencing great difficulty, since the sides of the well were damp and slippery.

For every minute of effort, the cat gained three feet. It was then too tired to struggle further and rested. During that next minute of rest, the cat slid back two feet.

How long did it take the cat to get out of the well?

Answer on page 153

THE PROBLEM OF THE LADY AND THE TIGER

In ancient days, a certain crafty king had a daughter as beautiful as he was vicious. Her charm and beauty attracted suitors from the four corners of the earth who came to sue for her hand.

But the king imposed harsh conditions. Each suitor was obliged to put up a fortune, if he even dared to try to win the maiden, a fortune which became forfeit to the crown if the suitor was unsuccessful. Then the candidate was given a number of difficult feats to perform. If he succeeded in overcoming these trials of strength and courage, he would then be led to a box which contained two slips of paper. On one there was written the name of the princess; on the other, the word *Tiger*. If he drew the slip with the word *Tiger* on it, he would be thrown into a cage, there to meet a cruel death.

Mathematically, his chances of winning the girl were even; but practically, his chances were nil because the unscrupulous monarch always put into the box two slips of paper on both of which was written the word *Tiger*.

After many suitors had met an untimely death in this manner, the princess had become aware of her father's deceit.

One day, a handsome young man came a-riding to the palace, and she immediately fell in love with him. Since she couldn't bear to see him be torn limb from limb by a vicious tiger, she told him of the king's stratagem and what lay in store for anyone who tried for her hand.

Undaunted, the young man announced that he was a suitor, and accomplished the feats of strength and other tasks set for him. Then he was led away to the box which held his fate.

But somehow he contrived to outwit the king. How did he do it?

Answer on page 153

THE PROBLEM OF THE COUNTERFEIT COIN

A king of ancient days once wished to reward one of his wise men, so he had his servants lay before the sage nine coins and a balance scale.

Addressing the object of his largesse, the king said, "There are nine coins here. Eight of them are made of pure gold. One of them has been debased by a lesser metal, which of course, does not weigh as much as gold.

"Now," continued the king, "you will determine your own reward. If you weigh each coin separately, you will, of course, find out which coin weighs the least, and that one will obviously be the counterfeit coin. But if you proceed in that manner you will be obliged to use the balance scale nine times. You would then achieve the worst result, for every time you use the scale, you lose one coin. You can take 15 minutes to think over how to proceed. Since you are a very wise man, you will manage to use the balance scale the fewest possible number of times."

The sage retired for a few minutes, and then came back and addressed himself to the king. "Sire," he said, "I am now ready to pick the counterfeit coin." And he proceeded to do this, using the scale the least number of times necessary to determine which of the nine coins was the counterfeit.

How did he contrive to find out? How many times did he use the scale?

Answer on page 154

THE PROBLEM OF THE BEAR

Sir Burton McBurton, the famed sportsman, told this story to his comrade, Sir John McJohn: Sir Burton left his camp on a hunting expedition. He trudged three miles due south, at which point he spied a fine bear. He took careful aim, shot, and the prize was his.

Leaving his kill where it had fallen, he marched on five miles due east in quest of further game. At this point he found that he was but three miles away from where he first started.

Sir John was not interested in finding out how far Sir Burton walked that day. Oddly, all he asked was, "What color was the bear?" Sir Burton, upset at his comrade's obtuseness, told him to figure it out himself. What answer should Sir John have arrived at?

Answer on page 154

THE PROBLEM OF THE TRAINS

A train leaves New York every hour on the hour. A train leaves Washington every hour on the hour. Both trains run on Eastern Standard time. It takes six hours for the trip from New York to Washington. It takes six hours from Washington to New York.

You are on a train which leaves New York for Washington at eleven in the morning. As your train pulls out of Penn Station in New York, a train from Washington is just gasping out its last chug as it slowly comes to a halt.

Including this incoming train, how many trains will you see en route from New York to Washington throughout your trip? It is assumed, of course, that you do not fall asleep, that no cinders get in your eye, and that, in fact, you do nothing else but concentrate on the solution of this problem.

Answer on page 154

THE PROBLEM OF THE BOOKWORM

Dr. James Farnol, a professor of literature, was entertaining a crony, Professor Algernon Guthrie. The talk veered to the Elizabethan drama. To prove a point, Dr. Farnol took down two dusty, calfskin-bound volumes of Beaumont and Fletcher. The edition was at least two hundred years old, and he had not touched these particular books for about thirty-five years. He was not particularly amazed when he found that the pages of the books were mildewed, and that a worm had eaten its way from Page one of Volume One to the last page of Volume Two.

Professor Guthrie, being a scientific man, determined to compute exactly how far the worm had traveled. He measured the books carefully, and found that each book was exactly one inch thick, not counting the thickness of the binding, and that the cover of each book was one eighth of an inch thick. In less than a minute he told Dr. Farnol just how much space the worm had eaten through.

At what result did Professor Guthrie arrive?

Answer on page 154

THE PROBLEM OF THE FORTY-TWO BEERS

In Guatelavia, the standard dollar is worth 100¢. In the bordering country of Tinto, the standard dollar is also worth 100¢. In fact, both dollars contain the same gold equivalent and are of exact value.

However, because of conditions of foreign exchange, the Guatelavian dollar is worth only 90¢ in Tinto, while the Tintoese dollar is worth but 90¢ in Guatelavia.

One day a smart Yankee with an enormous thirst drops into a Guatelavian cafe and orders a 10¢ beer. He hands over the single Guatelavian dollar that he has in his pocket, and he asks for 90¢ in change in Tintoese money. Since the Tintoese dollar is only worth 90¢ in Guatelavia, the barkeep gives him a full Tintoese dollar.

Whereupon our friend hops across the border and makes for the nearest saloon. He orders a beer and hands the bartender in Tinto a Tintoese dollar—the one he got in Guatelavia—demanding 90¢ change in Guatelavian money. Since, as aforesaid, the Guatelavian dollar is worth only 90¢ in Tinto, he receives a full Guatelavian dollar for his change.

Things look pretty bright for the Yankee, and he keeps up the transaction the whole day long, imbibing exactly 42 beers. When he is done, he finds that he has the same Guatelavian dollar that he started out with.

Now apparently the Guatelavian cafe sold 21 beers at the ordinary price and made a profit; and apparently the Tintoese saloon sold 21 beers with a profit, and evidently the American financial wizard got 42 beers without expending a single penny. . . . So the question remains: "Who paid for them there beers?"

Answer on page 155

THE PROBLEM OF THE BLIND MAN

Three men are seated around a circular table facing each other. They are told that a box in the room contains five hats —three white and two black. A hat is placed on each man's head. The remaining two hats are unseen. No man sees the hat that is placed on his own head.

One man is then asked what color hat he believes to be on his head. He looks at the other two hats on the heads of his companions, and then says he doesn't know.

The second man, in reply to a similar question, admits that he too doesn't really know.

The question is then put to the third man, *who is blind*. He correctly announces the color of the hat on his head.

Can you tell what color that hat was and can you outline the reasoning which the blind man followed?

Answer on page 155

THE PROBLEM OF THE TARDY GOLFER

(The trick in solving this problem is to achieve a solution without resorting to a trial-and-error method and without playing around with algebra. This problem can be solved by simple arithmetic. Use your noodle to reason it out logically.)

"Get out of that jalopy, you wretch!" John yelled, "You're two hours late and it will take us weeks to tee off the first green! A fine time to start for the course—ten o'clock!"

Mac stepped out of his car so dejectedly, so miserably, that John could not help but soften.

"What's up, Mac?"

"Darn the luck! I left at six on the dot."

"Six? You gave yourself only two hours to cover 120 miles?"

"Sure," replied Mac, "I've done it plenty of times. I can always figure on sixty miles per so early in the morning— fact is, that's just what I was averaging when out of nowhere this old tin can of mine developed stomach trouble. From then on I've been creeping along steady at fifteen miles per hour."

"Gee! Too bad! When did the old boiler start balking?"

Can you answer John's question?

Answer on page 155

THE PROBLEM OF THE MURDERESS

Two sisters were married, and with their husbands jointly occupied a single apartment. The men, apart from being brothers-in-law, were otherwise unrelated.

One night, while both men were asleep, one of the girls said to her sister: "Come with me." She led her into the chamber where the two men were sleeping, and having approached her own husband, she drew a dagger and plunged it into his vitals. He awoke, shouting in his death agony: "You are murdering me!"

The victim's brother-in-law, awakened by his cries, heard the woman announce coldly, "Yes, that's what I intend to do," and saw her again plunge the poniard up to its hilt into the victim's heart.

All the foregoing facts were established at the trial, not only by the evidence of the accused's sister and brother-in-law, but by the confession of the defendant herself. The jury duly brought in a verdict of "Guilty of murder in the first degree."

The judge stated that the verdict was unimpeachable, and while deploring the depravity of the defendant, he nevertheless stated to a crowded courtroom that under the law he found it impossible to pronounce sentence upon her. The accused then walked off scot-free.

Now take it for granted that the trial was held in due conformity with legal requirements. Take it for granted that the verdict could not be set aside for any legal technicality, and furthermore, take it for granted that the judge was fully competent and exercised unimpeachable judgment. In short, the difficulty did not arise from any deficiencies in either the processes of the law or the presiding tribunal. The dilemma arose solely out of the circumstances of the case.

What logical reason could the judge have for refusing to pronounce sentence upon the murderess?

Answer on page 156

THE PROBLEM OF THE DRY-GOODS DEALER

A dry-goods dealer has a five-yard piece of 36-inch-wide material. A lady wishes to purchase 1½ yards. Neither a yardstick nor a tape measure, nor any measuring device or box is available. How is the difficulty solved?

Answer on page 156

THE PROBLEM OF THE CIGARETTE BUTTS

It was one o'clock in the morning. All the boys had cleared out by this time, and Tom and Joe had settled down in comfortable armchairs to discuss the events of the evening. Tom reached into his cigarette pack only to find that it was empty. Joe had smoked his last cigarette 20 minutes ago. A quick search through the small apartment turned disappointment to dismay. There wasn't a cigarette to be found, and all the neighborhood stores were closed. And for Tom and Joe there was no such thing as a good talk without a good smoke.

Joe scurried around the apartment collecting butts. He came up with 25. The boys had some cigarette paper on hand. They found that the tobacco in five butts was sufficient to manufacture a new cigarette.

Assuming that Joe and Tom used all the tobacco in the house, how many cigarettes did they smoke?

Answer on page 156

THE PROBLEM OF THE STOLEN CAMEO

Sir Michael Farnsworth was elated. From some tumble-down shop in Leghorn he had brought back to England a cameo which he knew was a premier specimen. He presented his find for appraisal to Geoffrey Warren, senior member of Warren & Co., dealers in objets d'art for more than two hundred years. Mr. Warren, after careful scrutiny, acclaimed the carved piece a veritable masterpiece.

Sir Michael determined to deed the cameo to the British Museum.

Four days later, Sir Michael again appeared at Warren's. His gift had been accepted. The cameo needed furbishing. Geoffrey Warren stated that he himself would attend to the matter, for he would not entrust so precious a piece to any but his own practiced hands. The same afternoon, a reporter from *The Times* obtained a statement from Mr. Warren. The old gentleman, departing from the conservatism of years, pronounced the Farnsworth cameo to be the finest specimen extant.

Two days later, Scotland Yard was notified that the solid house of Warren & Co. had been despoiled of its greatest treasure. The Farnsworth cameo had been stolen. The police, after routine examination and routine questioning, rendered their routine report. Sir Michael was told that the house of Warren & Co. would stand by its loss. The cameo was worth £50,000—£50,000 would be paid.

But Sir Michael was shocked far beyond the thought of money. He had been robbed of fame. Secretly he engaged one of the most brilliant private detectives in London. Within three hours he was informed that Geoffrey Warren himself had stolen the cameo.

At first Sir Michael wouldn't believe it. The thought was preposterous. The man had been entrusted with millions during his long, honorable career. Furthermore, the cameo, publicized throughout the world of art, was the only one of its kind and could never be resold. A collector anywhere in the world would recognize it immediately. As to the idea that Geoffrey Warren had purloined the precious cameo simply for the joy of possession, that too was absurd. Had not Geoffrey Warren held within the palm of his hand for more than forty years the finest gems that existed? However, confronted with the accusation, Geoffrey Warren readily confessed.

The problem is to determine what motive impelled Mr. Warren to the theft of the cameo. The answer is not to be found in some extraneous circumstance, such as a personal grievance. A broad hint to the solution will be found in the fact that after the theft was discovered, Farnsworth and Warren remained good friends.

Answer on page 156

THE PROBLEM OF THE BLIND ABBOT

A medieval tale tells of a blind abbot who had twenty prodigal monks under his care. He and his charges lived in the top story of a square tower which was arranged in nine cells as illustrated. He himself occupied the center cell.

Each night it was his habit to patrol the abbey and to count his charges in order to make sure that the monks were all at home. His own peculiar method of tallying was to count nine heads for each wall. If he got a full count, he took it for granted that all were present.

Now a certain sly fellow arranged the beds so that two of the boys could leave of a night and make whoopee without the old codger suspecting any A.W.O.L.

On another night, this shrewd young fellow even contrived to bring in four comrades from a neighboring monastery for a party. He arranged the group so cleverly that when the abbot made his evening round, he still counted only nine heads along each wall.

A few months later, the boys decided to give a grand blowout. They increased the attendance to thirty-two, but still the abbot did not sense that anything was amiss.

And as a grand finale, they held one big gala super-affair, at which thirty-six monks attended, but still the blind abbot counted but nine heads along each wall.

Now the problem is to discover how that wily brother arranged the monks in each cell so that eighteen, twenty, twenty-four, thirty-two and thirty-six friars were present, although the blind abbot in each case counted nine heads along each wall of the tower.

Answer on page 156

THE PROBLEM OF THE HORSE TRADER

A horse trader brings a string of horses to a horse fair. As admission charge, he gives up one of his horses. At the fair, he sells one half of those remaining; and on the way out, he is charged one horse as a trading fee.

He proceeds to a second fair where like conditions prevail. There he pays one horse to get in, sells half of the horses he still has on hand, and pays a single horse as trading fee.

And, not content, he proceeds to a third fair. Here again he pays one horse to get in, sells one half the horses remaining, and is charged a single horse on the way out as a trading fee.

He then has one horse left on which to ride home with his proceeds.

How many horses did he start out with?

Answer on page 157

RUTHLESS RHYMES

The ditties below might well have been penned by the Marquis de Sade. Whoever is responsible for these shameless sentiments should at least find coal in his stocking next Christmas.

Little Willie, in the best of sashes,
Fell in the fire and was burned to ashes.
By and by the room grew chilly,
But no one liked to poke up Willie.

※

Making toast at the fireside,
Nurse fell in the grate and died;
And what makes it ten times worse—
All the toast was burned with Nurse.

※

Little Willie hung his sister;
She was dead before we missed her.
Willie's always up to tricks!
Ain't he cute? He's only six!

※

Pity now poor Mary Ames,
Blinded by her brother James;
Hot nails in her eyes he poked—
I ne'er saw Mary more provoked.

※

In the deep, deep drinking-well
    Which the plumber built her,
Dear Aunt Eliza fell—
    We must buy a filter.

Help! Murder! Police!
My wife fell down in grease;
    I laughed so hard, I fell in the lard.
Help! Murder! Police!

※

Baby Bobby in the tub;
Ma forgot to place the plug;
Oh what sorrow! Oh what pain!
There goes Bobby down the drain!

※

Sam had spirits naught could check,
    And today, at breakfast, he
Broke his baby sister's neck,
    So he shan't have jam for tea!

※

Little Willie, mean as hell,
Pushed his sister in the well,
Mother said, while drawing water,
"My it's hard to raise a daughter!"

Father heard his children scream,
So he threw them in the stream;
Saying, as he drowned the third,
"Children should be seen, *not* heard!"

❋

Nurse, who peppered baby's face
   (She mistook it for a muffin);
Held her tongue and kept her place,
   Laying low and sayin' nuffin';
Mother, seeing baby blinded,
Said, "Oh, nurse, how absent-minded!"

❋

O'er the rugged mountain's brow
   Clara threw the twins she nursed,
And remarked, "I wonder now
   Which will reach the bottom first?"

❋

Auntie, did you feel no pain
   Falling from that apple tree?
Would you do it, please, again?
   'Cos my friend here didn't see.

❋

I had written to Aunt Maud,
Who was on a trip abroad,
When I heard she'd died of cramp—
Just too late to save the stamp.

TRIPLE PLATFORM

Among the memorials of the sectional conflict of 1861-65 is an American platform which was arranged to suit all parties of that day. The first column is the *Secession* platform; the second, the *Abolition* platform; and the whole, read across in one line, presents the Democratic party platform of that particular era.

Hurrah for	The Old Union
Secession	Is a curse
We fight for	The Constitution
The Confederacy	Is a league with hell
We love	Free speech
The rebellion	Is treason
We glory in	A Free Press
Separation	Will not be tolerated
We fight not for	The Negro's freedom
Reconstruction	Must be obtained
We must succeed	At every hazard
The Union	We love
We love not	The Negro
We never said	Let the Union slide
We want	The Union as it was
Foreign intervention	Is played out
We cherish	The old flag
The stars and bars	Is a flaunting lie
We venerate	The *habeas corpus*
Southern chivalry	Is hateful
Death to	Jeff Davis
Abe Lincoln	Isn't the Government
Down with	Mob law
Law and order	Shall triumph

COMIC DICTIONARY

Acoustic   An instrument used in shooting pool.

Acquaintance   A person whom we know well enough to borrow from, but not well enough to lend to.

Ad Libber   A man who stays up all night to memorize spontaneous jokes.

Adolescence   The age between puberty and adultery.

Adult   A person who has stopped growing at both ends and started growing in the middle.

Advertising   A technique that makes you think you've longed all your life for something you've never heard of before.

After-Dinner Speaking   The art of saying nothing briefly. An occupation monopolized by men . . . women can't wait that long!

Afternoon   That part of the day spent figuring how we wasted the morning.

Alarm Clock   A device for awakening childless households.

Alcohol   A liquid good for preserving almost anything except secrets.

Alimony   The high cost of leaving.

Ambassador   An honest man sent abroad to lie for the commonwealth.   *Sir Henry Wotton*

Americans   People who insist on living in the present tense.

Angel	A pedestrian who forgot to jump.
Ant	A small insect that, though always at work, still finds time to go to picnics.
Baby	An alimentary canal with a loud voice at one end and no responsibility at the other.
Bachelor	A man who never makes the same mistake once.
Bank	An institution where you can borrow money if you can present sufficient evidence to show that you don't need it.

Ambrose Bierce

Barber Shop	A clip joint.
Bargain	A transaction in which each party thinks he has cheated the other.

Bathing Beauty	A girl who has a lovely profile all the way down.
Beach	A place where a girl goes in her baiting suit.

Beatnik   Santa Claus the day after Christmas.

Bigamy   One wife too many. Monogamy is the same.

Boaster   A person who, every time he opens his mouth, puts his feats in.

Bore   A guy with a cocktail glass in one hand, and your lapel in his other.

Boss of the Family   Whoever can spend ten dollars without thinking it necessary to say anything about it. *Robert Quillen*

Brassiere   An invention designed to make a mountain out of a mole-hill, and vice versa.

Brat   A kid that displays his pest manners.

Bridge   A card game in which a good deal depends upon a good deal.

Bridge Expert   One who can keep a kibitzer quiet all evening.

Broadway   New York's main artery—the hardened artery. *Walter Winchell*

Budget   A mathematical confirmation of your suspicions.

Bureaucrat   A man who shoots the bull, passes the buck, and makes seven copies of everything.

Busybody   One who burns a scandal at both ends.

Cauliflower   A cabbage with a college education.
Mark Twain

Chafing Dish   A pretty girl who has been stood up on a date.

Childish Game   One at which your wife beats you.

Classic   A book which people praise and don't read.

Classical Music   The kind that we keep hoping will turn into a tune.   *Abe Martin*

Committee   A body that keeps minutes and wastes hours.

Commuter   A traveling man who pays short visits to his home and office.

Conceit	A form of I-strain.
Consult	To seek another's approval of a course already decided upon. *Ambrose Bierce*
Counter- Irritant	A woman who looks at everything and buys nothing.
Criminal	A person with predatory instincts who has not sufficient capital to form a corporation. *Howard Scott*
Crook	A business rival who has just left the room.
Cynic	One who knows the price of everything and the value of nothing. *Oscar Wilde*
Darkroom	A place where many a girl with a negative personality is developed.
Dachshund	Half a dog high by a dog and a half long.
Dentist	A man who lives from hand to mouth.
Detour	The roughest distance between two points.
Diner	A restaurant where you can eat dirt cheap . . . but who wants to eat dirt?
Diplomacy	To do and say the nastiest things in the nicest way. *Isaac Goldberg*
Diplomat	A fellow who has to watch his appease and accuse.
Economy	A way of spending money without getting any fun out of it.
Education	The knowledge that a chorus girl gets by stages and that a college girl gets by degrees.

Efficiency Expert	A guy smart enough to tell you how to run your business and too smart to start his own.
Egotist	A person of low taste, more interested in himself than me.
Elderly Wolf	One who's not gonna lust much longer.
Epigram	A wisecrack that has played Carnegie Hall. *Oscar Levant*
Eunuch	One who is cut off from temptation.
Evolution	An unsuccessful attempt to produce a human being.
Expert	One who knows more and more about less and less. *Nicholas Murray Butler*
Falsies	Hidden persuaders.
Firmness	That admirable quality in ourselves that is detestable stubborness in others.
Fish	The animal that seems to go for a vacation about the same time most fishermen do.
Flashlight	A case in which to carry dead batteries.
Free Country	One in which there is no particular individual to blame for the existing tyranny.
Gardening	A labor that begins with daybreak and ends with backbreak.
Genealogy	Tracing yourself back to people better than you are. *John Garland Pollard*
Genius	One who can do almost anything except make a living.

Gentleman	A worn-out wolf.
Gold-Digger	A girl with a gift of grab.
Golfer	A man who hits and tells.
Good-Bye	What money says when it talks.
Gossip	A woman with a nice sense of rumor.
Grade Crossing	The meeting place of headlights and light heads.
Grandmother	The person you bring the baby to for an overmauling.
Happiness	A peculiar feeling you acquire when you're too busy to be miserable.
Highbrow	A person who enjoys a thing until it becomes popular.
Hollywood	A place where you live happily and get married forever afterward.
Home	A place to go when all the other joints are closed.
Honest Politician	One who when he is bought will stay bought.
Horse-Sense	A degree of wisdom that keeps one from betting on the races.
Hospital Room	A place where friends of the patient go to talk to other friends of the patient.
Hospitals	Places where people who are run down wind up.
Hotel Guest	A person who leaves his room only because he can't get it into his bags.
Husband	What's left of a sweetheart after the

nerve has been killed.

Indian Reservation   The home of the brave.

Jury   A group of 12 people selected to decide who has the better lawyer.

Linguist   One who has the ability to describe a beautiful girl without using his hands.

Litter   The result of literary efforts.

Los Angeles   Six suburbs in search of a city.

Madam   For whom the belles toil.

Marriage   An institution that starts with billing and cooing, but only the billing lasts.

Mayflower   A small ship on which several million Pilgrims came to America in 1620.

Meteorologist   A man who can look into a girl's eyes and tell whether.

Mistress   A cutie on the Q.T.

Mummy	An Egyptian who was pressed for time.
Neurotic	A person who has discovered the secret of perpetual emotion.
New Yorkers	A group of people who feel rich because they charge each other so much.
Night-Club Dancing	Merely lifting one's eyebrows in time to the music.
Nudist	A person who goes coatless and vestless, and wears trousers to match.
Oboe	An ill woodwind that nobody blows good.
Out of Bounds	A pooped kangaroo.
Overeating	An activity which will make you thick to your stomach.
Petition	A list of people who didn't have the nerve to say no.
Petting	A study of anatomy in braille.
Philosophical	The cheerful attitude assumed by everybody not directly involved in the trouble.
Popular Girl	One who has been weighed in the balance and found wanton.
Practical Nurse	One who marries a rich, elderly patient.
Procrastination	Putting off problems for a brainy day.
Prune	A plum that has seen better days.
Psychology	The science that tells you what you already know in words you can't understand.
Public Speaking	The art of diluting a two-minute idea with a two-hour vocabulary.

Punctuality	The art of guessing how late the other fellow is going to be.
Racehorse	An animal that can take several thousand people for a ride at the same time.
Radical	A conservative out of a job.
Regular Drinking	Drinking between drinks.
Repartee	An insult with its dress-suit on.
Resort	A place where the tired grow more tired.

Rummage Sale	A place where you can buy stuff from somebody else's attic to store in your own.
Salesmanship	The difference between rape and rapture.
Sales Resistance	The triumph of mind over patter.
Sex	The most fun you can have without laughing.
Shotgun Wedding	A case of wife or death.
Skeleton	A man with his insides taken out and his outsides taken off.
Smart Cooky	A girl who starts out with a little slip and ends up with a whole wardrobe.

Strength of Mind	A person who can eat one salted peanut.
Super Salesman	One who can sell a double-breasted suit to a man with a Phi Beta Kappa key.
Sympathy	That which one woman offers another in exchange for the details.
Tact	The ability to make your guests feel at home when you wish they were.
Titian	The color a poor red-headed girl's hair becomes as soon as her father strikes oil.
Traffic Light	A little green light that changes to red as your car approaches.
Untouchables	People you can't borrow money from.
Used Car	A car in first crash condition.
Vacation	A period during which people find out where to stay away from next year.
Washington	The only place in the world where sound travels faster than light.
Window Screen	A device for keeping flies in the house.
Wolf	A man who invites a girl for a scotch and sofa.
Yesmen	Fellows who hang around the man that nobody noes.

ANAGRAMS AND PALINDROMES

An anagram is, plain and simple, a rearrangement of the letters of a word or words to make another word or words. The word SMILE, for example, yields the anagram *slime*, as well as *miles* and *limes*.

One of the earliest and best-known anagrams was created from the question that Pilate asked Jesus:

Quid est veritas? [What is truth?]

THE ANSWER:
Est vir qui adest. [It is the man who is here.]

Here are some other unusually apt anagrams:

THE EYES	*They see.*
A SHOPLIFTER	*Has to pilfer.*
THE COUNTRYSIDE	*No city dust here!*
THE MONA LISA	*No hat, a smile.*
THE NUDIST COLONY	*No untidy clothes!*
THE UNITED STATES OF AMERICA	*Attaineth its cause: freedom!*

Many have been frustrated by the tricky task of making one word out of *new door*. If the solution eludes you, turn to *page 157*.

Anagrams have inspired linguistic jugglers to various creative efforts, for better or verse. To wit:

> *A* VILE *young lady on* EVIL *bent,*
> *Lowered her* VEIL *with sly intent.*
> *"*LEVI,*" she said, "It's time to play.*
> *What shall we do to* LIVE *today?"*
> *"My dear," said he, "do as you please.*
> *"I'm going to eat some* IVEL *cheese!"*

(Ivel cheese is a fictitious *fromage* made in the valley of the non-existent Ivel river.)

Consider the following quatrain in which the letters P T S and O have been used to form five different words:

> *Oh, landlord, fill our thirsting* POTS,
> *Until the* TOPS *flow over;*
> *Tonight, we* STOP *upon this* SPOT,
> *Tomorrow,* POST *for Dover.*

An anagram that reads the same backwards and forwards —the word *toot,* for instance—is called a palindrome.

The story goes that the first palindrome ever fashioned was uttered by the first man. Adam allegedly introduced himself to Eve thus;

"MADAM, I'M ADAM."

Here are a few small ones:

STEP ON NO PETS.

LIVE NOT ON EVIL.

DRAW, O COWARD!

'TIS IVAN ON A VISIT.

WAS IT A RAT I SAW?

YREKA BAKERY *(an actual bakery at*
322 W. Miner St., Yreka, California)

A palindrome of great historical interest is the classic supposedly uttered by Napoleon:

"ABLE WAS I ERE I SAW ELBA."

A palindrome that might be instrumental in celebrating a Black Mass is this exhortation to Satan:

LIVE, O DEVIL! REVEL EVER! LIVE! DO EVIL!

And here's one that offers a revolutionary method for keeping trim:

DOC, NOTE I DISSENT: A FAST NEVER PREVENTS
A FATNESS. I DIET ON COD.

But undoubtedly the cleverest palindrome ever penned in English was the work of some anonymous genius who apotheosized the Panama Canal in seven words which, however you look at them, yield the same pithy statement:

A MAN, A PLAN, A CANAL—PANAMA!

WHIMSICAL VERSE

The following stanzas, offered for your delectation, range in literary merit from slight to nil. Nevertheless, many have survived through generations which, in itself, attests to their appeal.

The savages closed around the tent;
    The lovers trembled in the gloom;
They knew their life was well-nigh spent,
    They knew they faced their doom.
He kissed the ringlets on her head,
    He crushed her in embrace of death;
And as he kissed her lips he said,
    "There's garlic on your breath!"

☀

If all the land were apple-pie,
    And all the sea were ink;
And all the trees were bread and cheese,
    What should we do for drink?

☀

Divorced are Mr. and Mrs. Howell;
He wiped their car with her guest towel.

If all be true that I do think,
There are five reasons we should drink;
Good wine—a friend—or being dry—
Or lest we should be by and by—
Or any other reason why.

Henry Aldrich

※

Yesterday upon the stair
I saw a man who wasn't there.
He wasn't there again today;
I wish to heck he'd go away.

※

I sneezed a sneeze into the air,
It fell to earth I know not where;
But hard and cold were the looks of those
In whose vicinity I snoze.

※

I eat my peas with honey,
    I've done it all my life;
They do taste kind of funny,
    But it keeps them on the knife.

Alas! the poor Hindu; he does what he kindu;
And as for his trousers, he makes his own skindu.

※

"I love the ground you walk on!" This was the tale he told.
For they lived up the Klondike, and the ground was full of
gold!

※

How sweet to waken in the morn
   Without a care the mind to cumber,
Then hurry to the phone and find
   Some jerk is calling the wrong number.

※

I crept upstairs, my shoes in hand,
   Just as the night took wing,
And saw my wife, four steps above,
   Doing the same darned thing.

※

Mary Jones took her skates
   Upon the ice to frisk;
Now wasn't she a foolish girl
   Her little *

I often pause and wonder at fate's peculiar ways,
For nearly all our famous men were born on holidays.

※

This is the story of Johnny McGuire
Who ran through the town with trousers on fire.
He went to the doctor's and fainted with fright
When the doctor told him his end was in sight.

※

Here is a riddle most abstruse:
 Canst read the answer right?
Why is it that my tongue grows loose
 Only when I grow tight?

※

The bee is such a busy soul
It has no time for birth control;
And that is why in times like these
There are so many sons of bees.

WORLD WAR I

The general got the croix-de-guerre—
And the son of a bitch was never there.

WORLD WAR III

I won't print and you won't see
The verses written on World War III.

※

"Come, come," said Tom's father, "at your time of life,
There's no longer excuse for thus playing the rake—
It is time you should think, boy, of taking a wife."
"Why so it is, father—whose wife shall I take?"

Thomas Moore

※

It isn't the cough
That carries you off;
It's the coffin
They carry you off in.

MATHEMATICAL ODDITIES

The Greek philosopher Pythagoras, famous to all students of geometry for his triangular theorem, was not the first man to be mystified by mathematics, but he was one of the most persistent in penetrating math's mysteries. If $a^2 + b^2 = c^2$, Old Pythy reasoned, perhaps there is more to numbers than meets the eye—so much, in fact, that the secret to existence itself might lie in numerology. With this observation, Pythagoras was elevated from philosopher and mathematician to seer and demi-god. His mathematical investigations led his followers to form a religious cult of substantial influence in classical Greece.

Now, it is problematical whether numbers are at the heart of the universe, and whether the smell of a flower can be expressed as a mathematical relationship. But numbers are certainly mysterious, and maybe even magical. Here are just a few of the innumerable puzzlers.

An unusually intriguing square may be formed out of 16 numbers, as shown in the diagram below. In this arrangement, the numbers in each vertical, horizontal, and diagonal row add up to 34.

What is more, the numbers in the four northwest squares add up to 34, as do the numbers in the southwest, northeast, and southeast quadrants. And if you total the numbers in the four center boxes, they too will come to 34.

1	15	14	4
12	6	7	9
8	10	11	5
13	3	2	16

Do you have a favorite digit (other than your fingers)? If so, then by doing the following multiplication, you can get that digit—nine times!

Suppose the number 6 is your pick. First, simply multiply 6 by 9. That gives you 54. Then write down the figure 123 45679. (Note that 8 is omitted.) Then multiply this number by 54. Here's what happens:

$$
\begin{array}{r}
12345679 \\
\times\ 54 \\
\hline
49382716\ \ \\
61728395\ \ \ \ \ \\
\hline
=\ 666666666
\end{array}
$$

You will get the same result with any other digit.

※

Now examine this multiplication marvel:

$$
\begin{aligned}
1 \times 9 + 2 &= 11 \\
12 \times 9 + 3 &= 111 \\
123 \times 9 + 4 &= 1111 \\
1234 \times 9 + 5 &= 11111 \\
12345 \times 9 + 6 &= 111111 \\
123456 \times 9 + 7 &= 1111111 \\
1234567 \times 9 + 8 &= 11111111 \\
12345678 \times 9 + 9 &= 111111111 \\
123456789 \times 9 + 10 &= 1111111111
\end{aligned}
$$

Isn't it a honey?

If you like the number 8, here's a simple way to produce it:

$$9 \times 9 + 7 = 88$$
$$9 \times 98 + 6 = 888$$
$$9 \times 987 + 5 = 8888$$
$$9 \times 9876 + 4 = 88888$$
$$9 \times 98765 + 3 = 888888$$
$$9 \times 987654 + 2 = 8888888$$
$$9 \times 9876543 + 1 = 88888888$$
$$9 \times 98765432 + 0 = 888888888$$

※

And here's an addition that yields a weird result:

	1	2	3	4	5	6	7	8	9
	9	8	7	6	5	4	3	2	1
	1	2	3	4	5	6	7	8	9
	9	8	7	6	5	4	3	2	1
+									2
2	2	2	2	2	2	2	2	2	2

※

No matter how big the number is that you multiply by 9, the digits in the answer will always add up to 9! You can do this with absolutely any number!

$$9 \times 78 = 702 \text{ and } 7 + 0 + 2 = 9$$
$$9 \times 568 = 5022 \text{ and } 5 + 0 + 2 + 2 = 9$$
$$9 \times 183 = 1647 \text{ and } 1 + 6 + 4 + 7 = 18,$$
$$\text{then } 1 + 8 = 9!$$

Many people think that we should not count by *10's* (the Decimal System) or by *12's* (Dozens). They say we should count by *9's*. That sounds hard, but only because we're not used to it. When you see some of the marvelous things that can be done with number 9, you may change your mind!

If you multiply any number by 9, the numbers that constitute the answer *will always add up to 9:*

$$9 \times 2 = 18 \text{ and } 1 + 8 = 9$$
$$9 \times 3 = 27 \text{ and } 2 + 7 = 9$$
$$9 \times 4 = 36 \text{ and } 3 + 6 = 9$$
$$9 \times 5 = 45 \text{ and } 4 + 5 = 9$$
$$9 \times 6 = 54 \text{ and } 5 + 4 = 9$$
$$9 \times 7 = 63 \text{ and } 6 + 3 = 9$$
$$9 \times 8 = 72 \text{ and } 7 + 2 = 9$$
$$9 \times 9 = 81 \text{ and } 8 + 1 = 9$$

You can get a lovely sort of pyramid effect when you multiply the numbers that follow:

$$1 \times 8 + 1 = 9$$
$$12 \times 8 + 2 = 98$$
$$123 \times 8 + 3 = 987$$
$$1234 \times 8 + 4 = 9876$$
$$12345 \times 8 + 5 = 98765$$
$$123456 \times 8 + 6 = 987654$$
$$1234567 \times 8 + 7 = 9876543$$
$$12345678 \times 8 + 8 = 98765432$$
$$123456789 \times 8 + 9 = 987654321$$

Here are some beautiful rows of figures you get when you multiply by 9 or multiples of 9:

987654321 ×   9 equals   8888888889
987654321 × 18 equals 17777777778
987654321 × 27 equals 26666666667
987654321 × 36 equals 35555555556
987654321 × 45 equals 44444444445
987654321 × 54 equals 53333333334
987654321 × 63 equals 62222222223
987654321 × 72 equals 71111111112
987654321 × 81 equals 80000000001

RIDDLES

The riddle is perhaps the oldest of all puzzles, and perhaps the most famous of all riddles is the one asked by the Sphinx:

> *What goes on four legs in the morning,*
> *on two at noon, and on three at night?*

Oedipus answered the riddle correctly, and thus became Oedipus Rex.

His solution: "Man. In infancy, he crawls; in his prime, he walks; in old age, he leans on a staff."

Another famous riddle is one that is reputed to have stumped Homer. Someone propounded these two lines to the bard:

> *What we caught we threw away;*
> *What we couldn't catch, we kept.*

The answer to this one is fleas.

It was a long time until the next classic riddle came along:

> *When is a door not a door?*

When it is ajar, naturally. What this riddle loses in classical phrasing it makes up in modern lunacy. Here are some more:

What is worse than a louse, stronger than God, and if you eat it you die?

> *Nothing. What is stronger than God? Nothing. What is worse than a louse? Nothing. And if you eat nothing—you die.*

What's the difference between a bird with one wing and a bird with two wings?

> *A difference of a pinion.*

I am the center of gravity, hold a capital situation in Vienna, and as I am foremost in every victory, am allowed by all to be invaluable. Always out of tune, yet ever in voice; invisible, though clearly seen in the midst of a river. I have three associates in vice, and could name three who are in love with me. Still it is in vain you seek me, for I have long been in heaven, and even now lie embalmed in the grave. Who am I?

> *The letter V.*

Four jolly men sat down to play,
And played all night till break of day;
They played for cash and not for fun,
With a separate score for every one;
Yet when they came to square accounts,
They all had made quite fair amounts!
Can you this paradox explain?
If no one lost, how could all gain?

> *They were musicians in a dance orchestra.*

What is the difference among a king's son, a monkey's mother, a bald head, and an orphan?

> *A king's son is an heir apparent, a monkey's mother is a hairy parent, a bald head has no hair apparent, and an orphan has nary a parent.*

Why are golfers not using clubs any longer?

> *Because they're long enough now.*

What has four wheels and flies?

> *A garbage truck.*

What did Cleopatra say when Mark Antony asked if she was true to him?

> *Omar Khayyam.*

YOU TELL 'EM

You tell 'em,	BALDHEAD	*You're smooth!*
You tell 'em,	BANK	*You're safe!*
You tell 'em,	BEAN	*He's stringing you!*
You tell 'em,	CABBAGE	*You've got the head!*
You tell 'em,	CASHIER	*I'm a poor teller!*
You tell 'em,	CHLOROFORM	*You put 'em to sleep!*
You tell 'em,	CLOCK	*You've got the time!*
You tell 'em,	CRYSTAL	*You're on the watch!*
You tell 'em,	DENTIST	*You've got the pull!*
You tell 'em,	DOUGH	*You're well-bred!*
You tell 'em,	ELECTRICITY	*You can shock 'em!*
You tell 'em,	ENVELOPE	*You're well posted!*
You tell 'em,	HUNTER	*I'm game.*
You tell 'em,	JUNE	*And don't July!*
You tell 'em,	MOUNTAIN	*I'm only a bluff!*
You tell 'em,	OPERATOR	*You've got their number!*
You tell 'em,	PIE	*You've got the crust!*

You tell 'em,	PRINTER	*I'm not your type!*
You tell 'em,	RAILROAD	*It's along your line.*
You tell 'em,	SIMON	*I'll Legree!*
You tell 'em,	DOCTOR	*You've got the patience!*
You tell 'em,	CEILING	*It's over my head.*
You tell 'em,	ENGLISH	*You're on the ball.*
You tell 'em,	PLATO	*It's Greek to me.*
You tell 'em,	TIN PAN	*It's up your alley.*
You tell 'em,	BIBLE	*You've got the word.*
You tell 'em,	SLEEPWALKER	*You never lie.*
You tell 'em,	TOOTH	*You've got the nerve.*
You tell 'em,	LAMP	*I'm in the dark.*
You tell 'em,	PLANE	*You're on the level.*
You tell 'em,	BALLOON	*You're on the up and up.*
You tell 'em,	NUMBER	*You're the one.*
You tell 'em,	CLOUD	*It's up to you.*
You tell 'em,	GOLDFISH	*You've been around the globe!*

TRACKS IN THE SNOW

WERE THE TRACKS IN THE SNOW CAUSED BY A PERSON OR PERSONS? AN OBJECT OR OBJECTS? AN ANIMAL OR ANIMALS? EXPLAIN JUST HOW THE TRACKS WERE MADE.

Answer on page 157

THE DARING YOUNG MAN

HOW DOES THE YOUNG MAN PROPOSE TO CROSS
THE BRIDGE SAFELY?

Answer on page 157

THE BLIND BUTLER

WHAT IS THE LEAST NUMBER OF SOCKS HE MUST BRING BACK?

Answer on page 157

THE ROPE LADDER

HOW MANY LADDER RUNGS WILL BE SUB-
MERGED TWO HOURS LATER?

Answer on page 157

THE SCALE PUZZLE

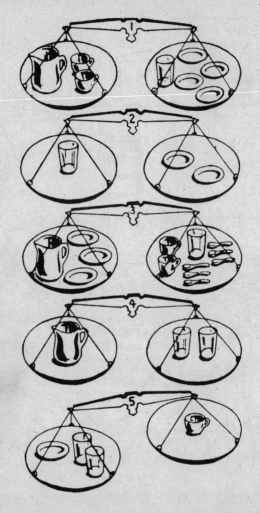

HOW MANY SPOONS SHOULD BE PLACED ON THE
RIGHT SIDE OF SCALE NO. 5 TO MAKE IT BALANCE?

Answer on page 157

PRIZE INSULTS

You have a bad habit ... *you breathe!*

※

Don't go away mad ... *just go away!*

※

THINK! *It may be a new experience!*

※

You can't be two-faced ... *or you wouldn't be wearing the one you've got!*

※

Don't think it hasn't been pleasant to meet you ... *because it hasn't!*

※

Why be difficult, when with just a little more effort you can be impossible!

※

What's on your mind? *If you will forgive the overstatement!*

※

You're a girl I should like to take home to mother ... *your* mother.

※

The sooner I never see your face again, the better it will be for both of us when we meet.

※

Use your head. *It's the little things that count!*

※

You should go a long way ... *and the sooner the better.*

I could grow to dislike you intensely . . . *but I'm not even going to bother.*

❊

If you have a minute to spare, tell me all you know.

❊

When I think of you I know it's not the heat—*it's the stupidity!*

❊

You're certainly trying . . . *very* trying!

❊

If a horse had your brains, he'd still be a horse.

❊

Go jump into the ocean and pull a wave over your head.

❊

Your visit has climaxed an already dull day.

❊

Why don't you come over and have dinner . . . *If you don't mind imposing!*

You've got a brain . . . *but it hasn't reached your head.*

※

I'd like to help you out . . . *Which way did you come in?*

※

I'm not in the habit of forgetting faces, but in your case I will make an exception.

※

You're a swell guy—*and you have a head to match!*

※

A day away from you is like a month in the country.

※

There is something about you that I like . . . *but you spent it.*

※

I couldn't warm up to you even if we were cremated together.

※

I can't think what I'll do without you, but it's worth a try.

※

Next time you pass my house, I'll appreciate it.

※

I wouldn't engage in a battle of wits with you. I never attack anyone who is unarmed.

※

I'm really pleased to see you're back, particularly after seeing your face.

RAPIER RIPOSTES

The ability to finish off a foe with precision and economy is as rare—and as prized—among wordsmiths as it is among militarists. There is, after all, no penalty in law for dealing a mortal blow to the pride of an adversary. The rapier riposte enables one to cut neatly yet deeply, to the amusement of all those in earshot—except the deserving victim, of course.

※

One classic example of slashing wit dates back to 18th-century England.

There was a great deal of ill feeling between William Pitt, First Earl of Chatham, and Robert Walpole, Earl of Orford. After a particularly heated speech by Pitt, Walpole, who felt enormously aggrieved, met Pitt outside Parliament and furiously declared, "Sir, you will either die on the gallows or perish from some unspeakable disease."

"That, my lord," rejoined Pitt, "depends upon whether I embrace your policies or your mistress."

※

About a century later, Dorothy Parker sat at a dinner party laughing at the antics of a wit who was something of a clown. Her neighbor, an overeducated young snob, was particularly disdainful.

"I'm afraid I can't join in the merriment," he scornfully remarked. "I can't bear fools."

"That's queer," observed Miss Parker, "your mother could."

※

Two American statesmen who seemed to be in constant antagonism were John Randolph and Henry Clay. At one time, after these bitter enemies had not spoken to one another for quite a while, they chanced to meet in a narrow street. It was evident that one would have to step aside to let the other pass.

Randolph firmly held his ground. "I never give way to scoundrels," he said.

Clay then stepped into the muddy gutter. "I *always* do," he replied.

❧

Calvin Coolidge, who was known for his taciturnity, had invited a large group of people to the White House for a social occasion. Among those who attended was the daughter of an Admiral, and the daughter of a European diplomat. The two girls, both in their early twenties, were talking to each other after the meal was served, and one of them commented upon the fact of how difficult it was to get to talk with the President.

"Oh," said the American girl, "I'm sure it can't be quite that difficult." The European young lady insisted that from everything she heard, it must be.

Whereupon the American girl said, "I'll bet I can get him to talk to me." And the lady from overseas loftily retorted, "I'll bet you ten dollars you couldn't get him to say three words."

"I couldn't!" replied the challenged young lady. "Well, I bet I could. You're on." And she peremptorily left her companion and strode over to where the President was standing, deep in contemplation.

When she thought the moment was opportune, she sidled up to Mr. Coolidge and said to him, "Mr. President, there's a young lady here from abroad who said you're the most difficult man in the world to talk to. She went so far as to bet me ten dollars that I couldn't even get three words out of you."

Coolidge looked her straight in the eye, and without a moment's hesitation, intoned, "You lose."

TYPOGRAPHICAL POETRY

A typographical poem may convey its message in both word and image, content and form—or it may communicate in a bizarre shorthand which yields surprising results. Offered here are some examples of each type of typographical verse. If you have any trouble deciphering the first ditty, here's a clue: the versifier might have taken lessons from Fanny Brice.

FUNEX?
SVFX
FUNEM?
SVFM
OK. LFMNX

ABCD goldfish?
LMNO goldfish
OSAR 2 goldfish!

O I C

I'm in a 10der mood to-day
    & feel poetic, 2;
4 fun I'll just — off a line
    & send it off 2 U.

I'm sorry you've been 6 0 long;
    Don't B disconsol8;
But bear your ills with 42de,
    & they won't seem to gr8.

YYUR
YYUB
ICUR
YY4ME

For a lark,
For a prank,
Ezra Shank
Walked a plank.
These bubbles mark
O
O
O
O
O
Where Ezra sank.

And what mean all these mysteries to me
    Whose life is full of indices and surds?
$x^2 + 7x + 53$
    $= 11/3$

Lewis Carroll

HOW'S BUSINESS?

Here are some likely responses to the above question by various tradesmen.

SAID THE SAILOR:	*Knot bad.*
SAID THE COFFEE SALESMAN:	*It's a grind.*
SAID THE DRUMMER:	*It's hard to beat.*
SAID THE SCULPTOR:	*Things are shaping up.*
SAID THE TEACHER:	*My work is classy.*
SAID THE ZOO KEEPER:	*It's beastly!*
SAID THE FLOOR WAXER:	*Going smoothly.*
SAID THE DAIRY FARMER:	*Cheesy, in a whey.*

SAID THE ASTRONOMER:	*Things are looking up.*
SAID THE DRESSMAKER:	*Just sew-sew.*

SAID THE DEMOLITION WORKER:	*Smashing!*
SAID THE COUNTERMAN:	*Pretty crummy.*
SAID THE COUNTERFEITER:	*We're forging on.*
SAID THE ICEMAN:	*Not so hot.*
SAID THE GRAVEDIGGER:	*Monumental!*
SAID THE DEEP-SEA DIVER:	*I'm about to go under.*
SAID THE TOBACCONIST:	*It's a drag.*
SAID THE STREETCLEANER:	*Things are picking up.*
SAID THE PIANIST:	*Right on key.*
SAID THE BULLFIGHTER:	*In the red.*
SAID THE GUNSMITH:	*Booming!*
SAID THE BOTANIST:	*Everything's coming up roses.*
SAID THE BARTENDER:	*It's been pretty tight lately.*
SAID THE LOCKSMITH:	*Everything's opening up.*
SAID THE SEWER WORKER:	*I've been getting to the bottom of things.*
SAID THE MUSICIAN:	*Nothing of note has been happening.*
SAID THE BAKER:	*I've been making a lot of dough lately.*
SAID THE TREE SURGEON:	*I've some shady deals going.*
SAID THE PILOT:	*Pretty much up in the air.*
SAID THE PHOTOGRAPHER:	*Everything is clicking— and developing well.*

SPOONERISMS

William Archibald Spooner was a British clergyman who lived from 1844 to 1930. He was a very nice man, but probably a little self-conscious. Very often, when he was speaking or lecturing, he would unwittingly switch his words around. His mistakes, which caused much laughter, have made him immortal.

On one occasion, Spooner, intending to announce to his congregation that they were about to sing the hymn "From Greenland's Icy Mountains," declared the title to be "From Iceland's Greasy Mountains."

This kind of mistake, switching around letters and thus changing the words, is called a spoonerism. Here are some others:

> Shores of skells were fired in a bittle batter.
>
> The picture is available in color and whack and blight.
>
> Shellout falters.
>
> He is a newted nose analyst.
>
> President Hoobert Heever.
>
> The Duck and Dooches of Windsor.
>
> The sporks and foons.
>
> You hissed my mystery lectures.
>
> The kankering kongs.
>
> A blushing crow.
>
> The tons of soil.
>
> His sin twister.
>
> Outside, a roaring pain is falling.

I am grattered and flatified.

A half-warmed fish.

"Kinquering Kongs Their Titles Take"

"Is it kisstomary to cuss the bride?"

It is reported that Spooner once referred to Queen Victoria as "our queer old dean."

Perhaps the most famous spoonerism is apocryphal. The story goes that the good reverend walked over to a lady in church and said, "Mardon me, padam, but this pie is occupewed. May I sew you to another sheet?"

Some vaudeville comic dreamed up this Spooneristic routine for a drunk:

"Now missen, lister, all I had was tee martoonis. Sough I theem under the affluence of inkahol, I'm not palf as hickled —half as packled—as thinkle peep—as theeple pink I am."

CURSES

In the Gay Nineties, curses were very fashionable and explicit. But in the cartoon strip, *Desperate Desmond,* where children's tender minds were to be protected, the villain could only grit his teeth and snarl at the hero, "Curses on you."

Here is a list of special beauties that we think you will find delicious—the crème de la crème of maledictions:

May you spend the best part of your day sitting on a soft chair ... my dentist's.

May you be the proof that man can endure everything.

Break a leg and lose your crutch.

May you be a liar with a poor memory.

Avoid old age ... go hang yourself.

Go take a long sleep and dream only of troubles.

May you lose all your teeth except one——the one that has the toothache.

May you become so poor that you have to go around begging, and I hope you have to come to me for alms, and I hope I have nothing to give you.

Take a nice walk and stumble on a skunk.

❊

May all your relatives move in on you.

❊

May you romp with joy and skip right into a sewer.

❊

May student barbers practice on your beard.

❊

May all your baths be too hot and your women too cold.

❊

May everything you cook stick to the bottom of the pot.

❊

May you become famous—in medical history.

LIMERICKS

The limerick is now an abiding part of our literature. A highly disciplined verse form, compact and clever, it tells a story in only five lines. Unlike most basic forms of English verse, such as the sonnet and the triolet, the limerick was not borrowed from other countries but is indigenously English, perhaps the only form in poetry that can be claimed to be an original English creation.

Undoubtedly, the limerick is the most quoted of all verse forms extant today. From the drawing room to the classroom, whether recited in a surreptitious whisper or blared forth uproariously, the limerick has captivated almost every echelon of society. Popular everywhere, it has especially become the darling of the intellectual.

The limerick reflects the temper of its day. Additions to this great fund of versification have been made by outstanding poets and publicists. Some of the most widely recited limericks have been ascribed, perhaps apocryphally, to Alfred Lord Tennyson, Norman Douglas, Eugene Field, Don Marquis, Heywood Broun, Woodrow Wilson, among others.

Back in the 1860's Edward Lear penned these rhythmical five-line ditties for children. But the form soon bounded out of the nursery onto the campus; and from there into the market place, the counting house, and the army. Once out on the streets and in full contact with the foibles, frustrations, and fantasies of the common folk, the limerick began to reflect the thoughts of the people more and more plainspokenly. The more pungent, punchy, and bawdy, the more easily were these verses remembered, and the more frequently were they quoted.

The limerick packs laughs anatomical
Into space that is quite economical.
    But the good ones I've seen
    So seldom are clean
And the clean ones so seldom are comical.

⚘

The limerick, peculiar to English,
Is a verse form that's hard to extinguish.
    Once Congress in session
    Decreed its suppression
But people got around it by writing the last
    line without any rhyme or meter.

⚘

There was a young lady named Banker,
Who slept while the ship lay at anchor;
    She awoke in dismay
    When she heard the mate say:
"Now hoist up the topsheet, and spanker!"

There was a young lady named Bright,
Who traveled much faster than light.
  She started one day
  In the relative way,
And returned on the previous night.

❋

There was a faith-healer in Deal
Who said, "Although pain isn't real,
  If I sit on a pin
  And it punctures my skin,
I dislike what I fancy I feel."

❋

A man to whom illness was chronic,
When told that he needed a tonic,
  Said, "Oh, Doctor, dear,
  Won't you please make it beer?"
"No, no," said the Doc, "that's Teutonic."

❋

There was a young maid from Madras,
Who had a magnificent ass;
  Not rounded and pink,
  As you probably think—
It was gray, had long ears, and ate grass.

❋

There was an old party of Lyme,
Who lived with three wives at one time.
  When asked, "Why the third?"
  He replied, "One's absurd,
And bigamy, sir, is a crime!"

Another young poet in China
Had a feeling for rhythm much fina.
　　His limericks tend
　　To come to an end
Quite suddenly.

※

There was a young lady named Maud,
A very deceptive young fraud;
　　She never was able
　　To eat at the table,
But out in the pantry—*O Lord!*

※

Said the chemist: "I'll take some dimethyloximidomesorala-
　　mide
And I'll add just a dash of dimethylamidoazobensaldehyde;
　　But if these won't mix,
　　I'll just have to fix
Up a big dose of trisodiumpholoroglucintricarboxycide.

God's plan made a hopeful beginning
But man spoiled his chances by sinning.
We trust that the story
Will end in God's glory—
But at present the other side's winning.

❋

There was a young fellow named Wier,
Who hadn't an atom of fear.
He indulged a desire
To touch a live wire.
(Most any last line will do here!)

❋

There's a wonderful family, called Stein,
There's Gert and there's Epp and there's Ein;
Gert's poems are bunk,
Epp's statues are junk,
And no one can understand Ein.

❋

As a beauty I am not a star,
There are others more handsome by far;
But my face—I don't mind it,
Because I'm behind it;
It's the people in front that I jar.
                        Anthony Euwer

❋

There was a young man of Japan
Whose limericks never would scan.
When someone asked why
He replied with a sigh,
"It's because I always try to get as many words
into the last line as I possibly can."

I wish that my room had a floor
I don't so much care for a door,
    But this walking around
    Without touching the ground
Is getting to be quite a bore!

☀

There was an Old Man of St. Bees
Who was stung in the arm by a wasp.
    When asked, "Does it hurt?"
    He replied, "No, it doesn't,
But I thought all the while 'twas a hornet."

                 W. S. Gilbert.

☀

There was a young man of Devizes,
Whose ears were of two different sizes;
    The one that was small
    Was of no use at all,
But the other won several prizes!

☀

An epicure dining at Crewe
Found quite a large mouse in the stew;
    Said the waiter, "Don't shout
    And wave it about
Or the rest will be wanting one too!"

WISECRACKS

The new army rifle weigh 8.60 pounds. After you've carried it for a few hours, the decimal point drops out.

꙼

The food in this hotel is absolutely poison—and such small portions!

꙼

Marriage is popular because it combines the maximum of temptation with the maximum of opportunity.

G. B. Shaw

꙼

Seven days in a jeep makes one weak.

꙼

Many a pert girl goes out to flirt and comes back *ex*-pert.

꙼

I know the King's English, and so is the Queen.

꙼

A great many prominent family trees were started by grafting.

What can one expect of a day that begins with getting up in the morning?

※

People are more fun than anybody.

Dorothy Parker

※

All work and no play makes jack.

※

I was in a phone booth talking to my girl, but someone wanted to use the phone, so we had to get out.

※

There are several good five-cent cigars on the market, but they are sold at higher prices.

※

After two days in the hospital, he took a turn for the nurse.

※

Getting the baby to sleep is hardest when she's about 18 years old.

Try praising your wife, even if it does frighten her at first.

Billy Sunday

❋

Look pleasant, please. As soon as I snap the picture, you can resume your natural expression.

❋

Every woman likes to be taken with a grain of assault.

❋

Money isn't everything—that is, *Confederate* money.

❋

He reminds me of the man who murdered both his parents and then when sentence was about to be pronounced, pleaded for mercy on the grounds that he was an orphan.

Lincoln

❋

The race is not always to the swift, nor the battle to the strong, but that's the way to bet.

Damon Runyon

A gossip is a woman with a good sense of rumor.

※

The average man is an irrational creature who's always looking for home atmosphere in a hotel, and hotel service at home.

※

The only thing worse than being talked about is not being talked about.

Oscar Wilde

※

A bachelor is a man who never makes the same mistake once.

※

Some taverns don't serve women at the bar: you have to bring your own.

※

Economy, my son, is anything your mother wants to buy.

Fred Neher

※

The cook was a good cook, as cooks go; and as cooks go, she went.

If all the college boys who sleep in class were placed end to end, they would be more comfortable.

※

The bigger the summer vacation, the harder the fall.

※

When people go to summer hotels for a change and rest, the bellboys get the change and the hotel gets the rest.

※

Money isn't everything—but it's ahead of whatever is in second place.

※

Half the lies they tell about me aren't true.

※

To love oneself is the beginning of a lifelong romance.
Oscar Wilde

※

It was just a platonic friendship—play for him, tonic for her!

※

You should study the Peerage . . . It is the best thing in fiction the English have done.
Oscar Wilde

After a divorce, a woman feels like a new man.

※

Youth is a wonderful thing. What a crime to waste it on children.
G. B. Shaw

※

Most women claim to be dresstitute.

There are three kinds of lies: lies, damned lies, and statistics.

Disraeli

※

My sister got herself a second lieutenant—the first one got away.

※

Never break your bread or roll in your soup.

※

In the first place God made idiots. This was for practice. Then He made School Boards.

Mark Twain

※

Where there's a will, there's a relative.

PARODIES

"Imitation is the sincerest form of flattery," wrote Charles Caleb Colton in the early 19th century. The parodies which follow are among the cleverest ever penned in the English language. Utterly delightful, all of them were written over half a century ago; and all of them have withstood the onslaught of time. The charm of these pieces has never withered.

AFTER LONGFELLOW

He killed the noble Mudjokivis.
Of the skin he made him mittens,
Made them with the fur side inside,
Made them with the skin side outside.
He, to get the warm side inside,
Put the inside skin side outside;
He, to get the cold side outside,
Put the warm side fur side inside.
That's why he put the fur side inside,
Why he put the skin side outside,
Why he turned them inside outside.

THE POETS AT TEA

Macaulay, who made it ⸺

Pour, varlet, pour the water,
    The water steaming hot!
A spoonful for each man of us,
    Another for the pot!
We shall not drink from amber,
    Nor Capuan slave shall mix
For us the snows of Athos
    With port at thirty-six;

Whiter than snow the crystals,
   Grown sweet 'neath tropic fires,
More rich the herbs of China's field,
The pasture-lands more fragrance yield;
For ever let Britannia wield
   The tea-pot of her sires!

Tennyson, who took it hot —

I think that I am drawing to an end:
For on a sudden came a gasp for breath,
And stretching of the hands, and blinded eyes,
And a great darkness falling on my soul.
O Hallelujah! . . . Kindly pass the milk.

Swinburne, who let it get cold —

As the sin that was sweet in the sinning
   Is foul in the ending thereof,
As the heat of the summer's beginning
   Is past in the winter of love:
O purity, painful and pleading!
   O coldness, ineffably gray!
Oh, hear us, our handmaid unheeding,
   And take it away!

Cowper, who thoroughly enjoyed it —

The cosy fire is bright and gay,
The merry kettle boils away
     And hums a cheerful song.
I sing the saucer and the cup;
Pray, Mary, fill the tea-pot up,
     And do not make it strong.

Browning, who treated it allegorically —

Tut! Bah! We take as another case—
   Pass the bills on the pills on the window-sill; notice the
      capsule
(A sick man's fancy, no doubt, but I place
    Reliance on trade-marks, Sir)——so perhaps you'll
Excuse the digression—this cup which I hold
    Light-poised—Bah, it's spilt in the bed!—well, let's on
      go—
Hold Bohea and sugar, Sir; if you were told
    The sugar was salt, would the Bohea be Congo?

Wordsworth, who gave it away —

   "Come, little cottage girl, you seem
      To want my cup of tea;
   And will you take a little cream?
      Now tell the truth to me."

   She had a rustic, woodland grin,
      Her cheek was soft as silk,
   And she replied, "Sir, please put in
      A little drop of milk."

   "Why, what put milk into your head?
      'Tis cream my cows supply";
   And five times to the child I said,
      "Why, pig-head, tell me, why?"

   "You call me pig-head," she replied;
      "My proper name is Ruth.
   I called that milk"——she blushed with pride—
      "You bade me speak the truth."

Here's a mellow cup of tea, golden tea!
What a world of rapturous thought its fragrance brings to me!
    Oh, from out the silver cells
    How it wells!
    How it smells!
Keeping tune, tune, tune
To the tintinnabulation of the spoon.
And the kettle on the fire
Boils its spout off with desire,
With a desperate desire
And a crystalline endeavour
Now, now to sit, or never,
On the top of the pale-faced moon,
But he always came home to tea, tea, tea, tea, tea,
      Tea to the n—th.

Rossetti, who took six cups of it —

    The lilies lie in my lady's bower
     (O weary mother, drive the cows to roost),
    They faintly droop for a little hour;
    My lady's head droops like a flower.

    She took the porcelain in her hand
     (O weary mother, drive the cows to roost),
    She poured; I drank at her command;
    Drank deep, and now—you understand!
     (O weary mother, drive the cows to roost.)

Burns, who liked it adulterated

Weel, gin ye speir, I'm no inclined,
Whusky or tay—to state my mind,
　　Fore ane or ither;
　For, gin I tak the first, I'm fou,
　　And gin the next, I'm dull as you,
　　　Mix a' thegither.

Walt Whitman, who didn't stay more than a minute

One cup for my self-hood,
Many for you. Allons, camerados, we will drink together,
O hand-in-hand! That tea-spoon, please, when you've done
　　with it.
What butter-colour'd hair you've got. I don't want to be
　　personal.
All right, then, you needn't. You're a stale-cadaver.
Eighteen-pence if the bottles are returned.
Allons, from all bat-eyed formula.

Barry Pain

And here are two more, in another vein. The first is by
Ben King, the second by Swinburne.

IF I SHOULD DIE TO-NIGHT

If I should die to-night
And you should come to my cold corpse and say,
Weeping and heartsick o'er my lifeless clay—
　　If I should die to-night
And you should come in deepest grief and woe—
And say: "Here's that ten dollars that I owe,"
　　I might arise in my large white cravat
　　And say, "What's that?"
　　If I should die to-night

And you should come to my cold corpse and kneel,
Clasping my bier to show the grief you feel,
      I say, if I should die to-night
And you should come to me, and there and then
Just even hint 'bout paying me that ten,
        I might arise the while,
        But I'd drop dead again.

THE HIGHER PANTHEISM IN A NUTSHELL

One, who is not, we see; but one, whom we see not, is;
Surely, this is not that; but that is assuredly this.

What, and wherefore, and whence: for under is over and
    under;
If thunder could be without lightning, lightning could be
    without thunder.

Doubt is faith in the main; but faith, on the whole, is doubt;
We cannot believe by proof; but could we believe without?

Why, and whither, and how? for barley and rye are not
    clover;
Neither are straight lines curves; yet over is under and over.

One and two are not one; but one and nothing is two;
Truth can hardly be false, if falsehood cannot be true.

Parallels all things are; yet many of these are askew;
You are certainly I; but certainly I am not you.

One, whom we see not, is; and one, who is not, we see;
Fiddle, we know is diddle; and diddle, we take it, is dee.

THE PURPLE COW

At the end of the nineteenth century, there appeared in a San Francisco periodical called the *Lark* a poem entitled "The Purple Cow." Written by one of the *Lark*'s editors, Gelett Burgess, the whimsical verse caught on immediately, and proved to be Burgess' best-known work, though he continued to write for nearly fifty years more. "The Purple Cow" was so popular a piece of nonsense that it inspired a gaggle of imitations and parodies, the best of these by Carolyn Wells.

Below, we offer Burgess' original, followed by Miss Wells' conceptions of how several well-known poets would have treated the subject of "The Purple Cow."

Mr. Burgess:

> I never saw a Purple Cow,
> I never hope to see one;
> But I can tell you, anyhow,
> I'd rather see than be one.

Carolyn Wells:

JOHN KEATS:

A cow of purple is a joy forever.
Its loveliness increases. I have never
Seen this phenomenon. Yet ever keep
A brave lookout; lest I should be asleep
When she comes by. For, though I would not be one,
I've oft imagined 'twould be joy to see one.

WILLIAM WORDSWORTH:

She dwelt among the untrodden ways
    Beside the springs of Dee;
A Cow whom there were few to praise
    And very few to see.

A violet by a mossy stone
    Greeting the smiling East
Is not so purple, I must own,
    As that erratic beast.
She lived unknown, that Cow, and so
    I never chanced to see;
But if I had to be one, oh,
    The difference to me!

HENRY WADSWORTH LONGFELLOW:

The day is done, and the darkness
    Falls from the wing of night
As ballast is wafted downward
    From an air-ship in its flight.

I dream of a purple creature
    Which is not as kine are now;
And resembles cattle only
    As Cowper resembles a cow.

Such cows have power to quiet
    Our restless thoughts and rude;
They come like the Benedictine
    That follows after food.

LORD TENNYSON:

Ask me no more. A cow I fain would see
    Of purple tint, like to a sun-soaked grape—
    Of purple tint, like royal velvet cape—
But such a creature I would never be—
        Ask me no more.

JOHN MILTON:

Hence, vain, deluding cows.
    The herd of folly, without colour bright,
    How little you delight,
    Or fill the Poet's mind, or songs arouse!
    But, hail! thou goddess gay of feature!
    Hail, divinest purple creature!
    Oh, Cow, thy visage is too bright,
    To hit the sense of human sight.
    And though I'd like, just once, to see thee,
    I never, never, never'd be thee!

ROBERT BROWNING:

All that I know
    Of a certain Cow
Is it can throw,
    Somewhere, somehow,
Now a dart of red,
    Now a dart of blue
(That makes purple, 'tis said).
    I would fain see, too.
This Cow that darkles the red and the blue!

PERCY BYSSHE SHELLEY:

Hail to thee, blithe spirit!
    Cow thou never wert;
But in life to cheer it
    Playest thy full part
In purple lines of unpremeditated art.

The pale purple colour
    Melts around thy sight
Like a star, but duller,
    In the broad daylight.
I'd see thee, but I would not be thee if I might.

We look before and after
    At cattle as they browse;
Our most hearty laughter
    Something sad must rouse.
Our sweetest songs are those that tell of Purple Cows.

DANTE GABRIEL ROSSETTI:

The Purple Cow strayed in the glade;
    (Oh, my soul! but the milk is blue!)
She strayed and strayed and strayed and strayed
    (And I wail and I cry Wa-hoo!)

I've never seen her—nay, not I;
    (Oh, my soul! but the milk is blue!)
Yet were I that Cow I should want to die.
    (And I wail and I cry Wa-hoo!)
    But in vain my tears I strew.

THOMAS GRAY:

The curfew tolls the knell of parting day,
    The lowing herd winds slowly o'er the lea;
I watched them slowly wend their weary way,
    But, ah, a Purple Cow I did not see.
Full many a cow of purplest ray serene
    Is haply grazing where I may not see;
Full many a donkey writes of her, I ween,
    But neither of these creatures would I be.

EDGAR ALLAN POE:

Open then I flung a shutter,
    And, with many a flirt and flutter,
In there stepped a Purple Cow which gayly tripped around
      my floor.
Not the least obeisance made she,
Not a moment stopped or stayed she,
But with mien of chorus lady perched herself above my door.
On a dusty bust of Dante perched and sat above my door.

And that Purple Cow unflitting
    Still is sitting—still is sitting
On that dusty bust of Dante just above my chamber door,
    And her horns have all the seeming
    Of a demon's that is screaming,
    And the arc-light o'er her streaming
Casts her shadow on the floor.
And my soul from out that pool of Purple shadow on the
      floor,
Shall be lifted Nevermore!

ALGERNON SWINBURNE:

Oh, Cow of rare rapturous vision,
    Oh, purple, impalpable Cow,
Do you browse in a Dream Field Elysian
    Are you purpling pleasantly now?
By the side of wan waves do you languish?
    Or in the lithe lush of the grove?
While vainly I search in my anguish,
    O Bovine of mauve!

Despair in my bosom is sighing,
    Hope's star has sunk sadly to rest;
Though cows of rare sorts I am buying,
    Not one breathes a balm to my breast.
Oh, rapturous rose-crowned occasion,
    When I such a glory might see!
But a cow of a purple persuasion
    I never would be.

JAMES WHITCOMB RILEY:

There, little Cow, don't cry!
    You are brindle and brown, I know.
        And with wild, glad hues
        Of reds and blues,
    You never will gleam and glow.
But though not pleasing to the eye
There, little Cow, don't cry, don't cry.

In the old ten-acre pasture,
    Lookin' eastward toward a tree,
There's a Purple Cow a-settin'
    And I know she thinks of me.
For the wind is in the gum-tree,
    And the hay is in the mow,
And the cow-bells are a-calling
    "Come and see a Purple Cow!"

But I am not going now,
    Not at present, anyhow,
For I am not fond of purple, and
    I can't abide a cow;
    No, I shall not go to-day,
    Where the Purple Cattle play.
    But I think I'd rather see one
    Than to be one, anyhow.

※

Riposte

Ah, yes, I wrote the "Purple Cow"—
    I'm sorry, now, I wrote it!
But I can tell you, anyhow,
    I'll kill you if you quote it.

Gelett Burgess

MALAPROPISMS

When what someone says is pertinent and to the point it may be said to be apropos. When it is the opposite of these things, it is malapropos.

In 1775, the year Richard Sheridan's comedy *The Rivals* was first presented, the world was given its model of linguistic maladroitness forevermore—the tongue-tied and muddle-headed Mrs. Malaprop. Her chronic misuse and abuse of the English language gave birth to the term *malapropism,* some choice examples of which are offered below.

Strategy is when you are out of ammunition but keep right on firing so that the enemy won't know.

※

If your father was alive, he'd be turning over in his grave.

※

Your whole fallacy is wrong!

※

Gender in English tells us if a man is male, female, or neuter.

※

Don't pay any attention to him—don't even ignore him!

※

The driver swerved to avoid missing the jaywalker.

Leo Rosten

※

He gets up at six o'clock in the morning no matter what time it is.

Leo Rosten

An oral contract isn't worth the paper it's written on.

Samuel Goldwyn

※

Don't blame God; He's only human.

Leo Rosten

※

Every man loves his native land whether he was born there or not.

Thomas Fitch

※

Let us be happy and live within our means, even if we have to borrow money to do it with.

Artemus Ward

※

You can observe a lot by watching.

Yogi Berra

※

Rome is full of fallen arches.

※

You've no idea what a poor opinion I have of myself, and how little I deserve it.

W. S. Gilbert

God bless the Holy Trinity.

> *A placard which actually led a parade of devout
> Catholics some years ago in Dublin.*

❋

The climate of the Sahara is such that its inhabitants have to
live elsewhere.

❋

I don't want any yesmen around me. I want everyone to tell
me the truth—even though it costs him his job.

> *Samuel Goldwyn*

❋

No one goes to that restaurant anymore; it's too crowded.

> *Yogi Berra*

❋

We're overpaying him, but he's worth it.

> *Samuel Goldwyn*

❋

A lot of people my age are dead at the present time.

> *Casey Stengel*

❋

Washington's farewell address was Mount Vernon.

> *Leo Rosten*

PUNS

Puns have been decried by some purer-than-thous as the lowest form of humor, but we agree with Edgar Allan Poe who wrote: "Of puns it has been said that those who most dislike them are those who are least able to utter them."

In any case, puns have been the darling of the literati for as far back as goeth the memory of man. Even Queen Elizabeth allegedly succumbed to the temptation when she told Lord of Burleigh:

> *"Ye be burly, my Lord of Burleigh, but ye shall make less stir in our realm than my Lord of Leicester."*

Other well-known personalities who have contributed to the lore of pundom, are:

GROUCHO MARX: When shooting elephants in Africa, I found the tusks very difficult to remove; but in Alabama, the Tuscaloosa.

F. P. ADAMS: Take care of your peonies and the dahlias will take care of themselves.

S. J. PERELMAN: Doctor, I've got Bright's disease and he's got mine.

SYDNEY SMITH: (upon observing two housewives yelling at each other across a courtyard): These women will never agree, for they are arguing from different premises.

PETER DE VRIES: The things my wife buys at auction are keeping me baroque.

F. P. ADAMS: Those Spanish senoritas are a snare Andalusian.

F. P. ADAMS: A group of Basques, fleeing before the enemy, were penned into a narrow mountain pass and wiped out. Which is what comes of putting all your Basques into one exit.

BENNETT CERF: A relative and namesake of Syngman Rhee, president of South Korea, was visiting our country to learn the magazine business, and got a job on what was at that time America's most popular picture periodical. On his first assignment, however, he lost himself in the mazes of New York City, until at last a Missing Persons Bureau investigator found him in a bar and cried: "Ah, sweet Mr. Rhee of *Life*, at last I've found you!"

And here are some delights from lesser-known punsters:

JIM HAWKINS: There's a vas deferens between children and no children.

JACK THOMAS: (Title for guidebook) Paris by Night and Bidet.

PHILIP GUEDALLA: (Reply to a slanderous attack on the Church): Any stigma will do to beat a dogma.

Four dons were strolling along an Oxford street one evening, discussing collective nouns: a covey of quail, an exaltation of larks, etc. As they conversed, they passed four ladies of the evening. One of the dons asked, "How would you describe a group like that?"

One suggested: "A jam of tarts?"
A second offered: "A flourish of strumpets?"

A third chimed in with: "An essay of Trollope's?"

Then the dean, the eldest and most scholarly of the four, apparently closed the discussion with: "I wish that you gentlemen would consider 'An anthology of pros.'"

Whereupon a voice behind them broke in with: "Surely you have overlooked the obvious: 'A pride of loins.'"

At a dinner party, the hostess-mother was listening with clearly evident delight to the compliments of a Mr. Campbell, which, by the way, the English pronounce by suppressing the "p" and the "b." Her daughter on the other hand was enthusiastically flirting with a gentleman named Nathaniel. Disturbed by her daughter's marked sprightliness, the mother frowned in severe reproach. Whereupon the daughter scribbled a note on a piece of paper and handed it to her mother:

Dear Ma, don't attempt my young feelings to trammel,
Nor strain at a Nat while you swallow a Campbell.

Well, as Clifton Fadiman states, of such puns we may say that their special virtue is to be tried and found wanton. Mr. Fadiman, however, has been guilty of penning the following:

In a Skid Row saloon, the patrons often enter optimistically and leave mistyoptically.

A combined charity drive represents an effort where everyone puts all their begs into one ask-it.

A gentleman crossing the English River Mersey and noting its muddy condition remarked, "Evidently the quality of Mersey is not strained."

Bennett Cerf tells of the man who poured pickle juice down a hill just to see if dill waters run steep.

And there was the wit who complained that he was always hearing his own stories told back to him: "A plain case of the tale dogging the wag."

These, then, are the rhymes that try men's souls. Before we submit our own dictionary of puns, we call Mr. James Boswell for the Defense:

> *A good pun may be admitted among the small excellencies of lively conversation.*

You may find the puns which follow perhaps less sophisticated, but nevertheless more uproarious.

AMAZON	You can pay for the eggs, but the amazon me.
ANTIDOTES	My uncle likes me very much and my antidotes on me.
ARREARS	Brother and I both hate to wash in back of arrears.
AVENUE	I avenue baby sitter.
AVOID	Stop me if you avoid this one before.
BULLETIN	My brother fought in the war and he has a bulletin his leg.
CANADA	You bring the corn and I'll bring a canada best peas.
CIGARETTE	Cigarette life, if you don't weaken.
CUCKOO	We have a new cuckoo makes nice cake.
DAISIES	Ma's always glad when school starts because Johnnie's such a nuisance the daisies at home.

DECEIT	Ma makes me wear pants with patches on deceit.
DEMURE	When people start to get rich, demure they get, demure they want.
DIABETES	That baseball team has sworn they'll either diabetes.
DIALOGUE	Insult her and you will dialogue a dog.
DUBLIN	Ireland is rich because its capital is always Dublin.
EURIPEDES	Mr. Tailor, Euripides pants and I'll make you pay.
EXPLAIN	Please don't scramble them; I like my explain.

FALSIFY	When I put a book on my head it falsify move.

FORFEIT	The horse jumped over the cop and landed with all its forfeit on the ground.
GLADIATOR	That old hen wasn't laying any eggs, so I'm gladiator.
HISTORIAN	That's historian he's stuck with it.
JUICY	When we came through the alley, juicy what I saw?
JUSTIFY	Ma promised me a quarter justify brush my teeth.
LAZINESS	It's no wonder baby doesn't get tired—he laziness crib all day.
LILAC	He's a nice kid but he can lilac anything.
MINIATURE	Take a pill and you'll be asleep the miniature in bed.
MUTILATE	I could get more sleep if our cat didn't mutilate every night.
NUISANCE	I haven't seen anything nuisance I came back.

REVEREND	Teacher says if I don't study I'll be in this grade for reverend ever.
SELFISH	That fish market would be just grand if it didn't make their men selfish.
SPADE	The man who digs ditches these days gets spade well for his work.
SURGEON	Willie likes his gray suit but he looks nicer with his blue surgeon.
TORONTO	When you hit the ball you have toronto first base.

UNAWARE	Every night, before I go to bed, I take off my unaware.
WIGGLE	She wears her hat all day because she's afraid her wiggle come off.

THE FARMER'S BEQUEST

A farmer dies and leaves a field in the shape shown below.

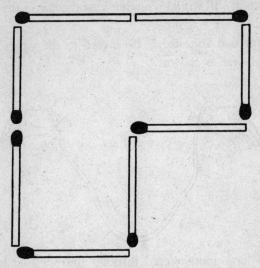

This field is represented by 8 matches, which should be set up in the manner shown. When the farmer dies, his will indicates that the field is to be divided into four equal parts, *each one of the same size and shape.*

You are given 4 matches to effect the division. How can such a division be made?

Answer on page 158

THE ROPE TRICK

This is really a great stunt, and a wonderful challenge for any group. It will work no matter what the age of the people involved.

Ask for two volunteers. Tie a cord to the wrists of one of the players as shown.

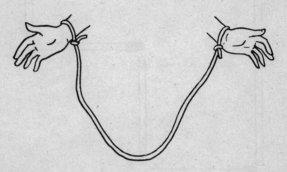

Now loop another cord through the one that has been tied, and tie the wrists of the second volunteer.

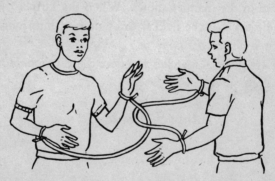

The challenge is for the two to extricate themselves without tearing, breaking, or unknotting the strings.

Believe it or not, it can be done, but the trials will be hilarious and it really won't be quite so easy. How is it accomplished?

Answer on page 158

PUT YOUR HEAD THROUGH
A CALLING CARD

This is a seemingly impossible stunt. Although it's easy to do, its effect is spectacular. All you need is an ordinary calling card, size 2″ by 3½″.

TIMOTHY T. BONES

34 Albemarle St.

Gravesend, Mass.

Then produce scissors, and challenge your audience to cut the card in such a way that anyone can put his head through the entire calling card without tearing it in any way.

Answer on page 158

SHOW ME

Show me where Stalin is buried—and I'll show you a Communist plot.

✻

Show me the first President's dentures—and I'll show you the George Washington Bridge.

✻

Show me a pharaoh who ate crackers in bed—and I'll show you a crummy mummy.

✻

Show me a squirrel's nest—and I'll show you the Nutcracker Suite.

✻

Show me Santa's helpers—and I'll show you subordinate clauses.

✻

Show me a famous surgeon—and I'll show you a big operator.

✻

Show me a cat that just ate a lemon—and I'll show you a sourpuss.

✻

Show me a cross between a fox and a mink—and I'll show you a fink.

✻

Show me a singing beetle—and I'll show you a humbug.

✻

Show me a famous composer's liquor cabinet—and I'll show you Beethoven's Fifth.

✻

Show me Eve's perfume—and I'll show you an Adam balm.

Show me a monarch who takes tea at four—and I'll show you the King's English.

❦

Show me a fowl with an artificial leg—and I'll show you a lame duck amendment.

❦

Show me a stolen sausage—and I'll show you a missing link.

❦

Show me a healed shaving scar—and I'll show you an old nick.

❦

Show me a frog on a lily pad—and I'll show you a toadstool.

❦

Show me a man who's afraid of Christmas—and I'll show you a Noel Coward.

❦

Show me a magician's notebook—and I'll show you a spell-binder.

Show me a man convicted of two crimes—and I'll show you a compound sentence.

※

Show me a one-word commercial—and I'll show you an adverb.

※

Show me two dozen satisfied rabbits—and I'll show you 24 carats.

※

Show me a burned-out post office—and I'll show you a case of blackmail.

※

Show me a cross between a cannon and a bell—and I'll show you a boomerang.

※

Show me a young lad's bed—and I'll show you a boycott.

※

Show me a wily halfback with a knack for sketching—and I'll show you an artful dodger.

※

Show me a workman who dismantles a roof—and I'll show you an eavesdropper.

※

Show me a baker who ran out of custard—and I'll show you a humble pie.

※

Show me a cross between a mule and a fox—and I'll show you a fool.

THE ANSWERS

THE ANSWERS

THE PROBLEM OF THE NOBLES AND THE SLAVES . . . Page 20

The first native must have said: "I am a noble." If he were in fact a noble, he would have told the truth and admitted it. On the other hand, if he were a slave, he would have lied and said that he was a noble.

The second native who said that the first one said he was a noble must have then been telling the truth. Therefore, he must be a noble. That means that his entire statement was true and therefore, it is conclusive that the first native was also a noble.

The third man, who says that the second one was a slave, is therefore obviously lying. He, then, must be a slave.

THE PROBLEM OF THE TELEPHONE CALL . . Page 21

On close consideration of the facts presented, it will become apparent that Winston's evident objective was to waken Malcolm solely for the purpose of *awakening him*. He never intended to communicate with him. Nor did he.

The only reason that Winston could have for wishing to accomplish his apparent mischief was that Malcolm, by sleeping, was doing *him* a mischief. You see, Winston and Malcolm were both tenants in the same apartment house, and Winston's bedroom adjoined Malcolm's. Malcolm was snoring so loudly that Winston couldn't fall asleep. The victim's only chance, which he cleverly saw, was to dis-

turb the disturber and beat him to the snooze.

THE PROBLEM OF THE MOAT . . . Page 22

Father arranged the two planks, as shown in the accompanying diagram.

THE PROBLEM OF THE DEAD TOURIST . Page 23

Seeing Mrs. Elkins' picture in the Boston society column, and reading the details of the tragic death of her husband, Mr. Harper remembered that Mrs. Elkins had been to his travel bureau to purchase tickets for a European trip. Examining the files, he discovered that she had bought one round-trip ticket and one one-way ticket. This led him to believe that she never expected Mr. Elkins to return.

THE PROBLEM OF THE STYMIED SAVAGE . Page 24

The missionary said: "I will die by fire."

If the voodoo man decided that this statement was a true one, execution would take place by shooting. That would make the statement false, and then the missionary would be consigned to the flames. But such a fate would definitely make the statement true, and then the missionary would have to be shot instead. The only way out of this dilemma was to let the clever cleric go.

THE PROBLEM OF THE PROFESSIONS . . Page 25

MR. GROCER IS THE BAKER.

MR. BUTCHER IS THE LAWYER.

MR. DOCTOR IS THE ARTIST.

MR. ARTIST IS THE BUTCHER.

MR. BAKER IS THE DOCTOR.

MR. LAWYER IS THE GROCER.

Analysis

Mr. Butcher, addressing Mr. Grocer, says that he heard that Mr. Grocer mashed his finger at his store under a tub of butter. Now, Mr. Grocer, having a store, is either a baker, a butcher, or a grocer. He cannot be a grocer because no man bears the name of his trade. A tub of butter would be found in a bakery but not in a butcher shop. *Therefore, Mr. Grocer is a baker.*

Mr. Artist cannot be either the doctor or the grocer because he would not refer to them in the third person, and Mr. Artist cannot be the baker because we have already established that Mr. Grocer is the baker. Mr. Artist cannot be the artist, because no man bears the name of his profession. Therefore, Mr. Artist must be either the lawyer or the butcher. We can be sure that he is not the lawyer because Mr. Doctor, while talking to him, mentions the lawyer, as if he were some

other person. *Therefore, Mr. Artist must be the butcher.*

Mr. Doctor states that he goes deep-sea fishing with the lawyer every week. Mr. Doctor cannot be the butcher or the baker because Mr. Grocer has already been established as the butcher. Again, the man who goes deep-sea fishing with the lawyer cannot be the doctor because it is Mr. Doctor who is talking and Mr. Doctor is not a doctor. Therefore, the lawyer goes deep-sea fishing with either the grocer or the artist.

But the lawyer does not go deep-sea fishing each week-end with the grocer who lives in Milwaukee. This fact becomes evident when it is realized that Milwaukee is situated inland more than 1,000 miles from either the East Coast or the West Coast of the United States and from the Gulf of Mexico. It would be impossible for a resident of Milwaukee to take a week-end trip each week to do deep-sea fishing. Therefore, by elimination, the lawyer goes deep-sea fishing with the artist. *This establishes Mr. Doctor as the artist.*

We still must determine who is the doctor, who is the lawyer, and who is the grocer. We can infer, however, that two of these men live in the same town.

The doctor lives in Milwaukee; the grocer lives in Milwaukee. The lawyer lives on the seacoast. Mr. Baker, talking to Mr. Lawyer, mentions that he got in a new interesting case at the office. He says that he will tell him about it during next week. This argues very strongly that Mr. Baker lives in the same city as Mr. Lawyer and not more than 1,000 miles away from him. It must be remembered that the Convention has been in session for a full week at St. Louis. Therefore, the lawyer presumably would leave for either the East Coast or the West Coast or the Gulf at the close of the Convention. In any event, his route home could not possibly take him through Milwaukee. Moreover, he has just seen his friends and has already taken a week's vacation and there is no reason to believe that he is going off another few hundred miles simply to visit. This reasoning points to the fact that the man who says so casually that he will drop in to tell Mr. Baker about his new interesting case during the week must be the doctor who lives with the grocer in Milwaukee. *This establishes the doctor as Mr. Baker, and the grocer as Mr. Lawyer.*

Of course, then, Mr. Butcher is the lawyer. His interest in the baker's mashed finger could have been actuated by other than professional motives. He could simply have been interested in determining how serious an accident his fraternity brother, the baker, had sustained. Moreover, since he has asked the baker to play golf with him during the week, it is very likely that they too, live near each other. There is nothing to indicate that the baker does not actually live in the same town with the lawyer.

THE PROBLEM OF THE TWO STUDENTS .   Page 26
They were two of a set of triplets.

THE PROBLEM OF THE TIRES .   .   .   .   Page 27
The car, of course, has four wheels, so that for a 27,000-mile journey it uses up 108,000 tire miles. Each tire is good for 12,000 miles, and math-

ematically *nine* tires will suffice.

The real problem is: How can the explorer get through the trip with this minimum number? The first four tires will be used up and discarded after 12,000 miles, one of the five remaining will have to be changed each 3,000 miles as follows: First 3,000 miles—Tires 1, 2, 3, 4; second 3,000 miles—Tires 2, 3, 4, 5; third 3,000 miles—Tires 3, 4, 5, 1; fourth 3,000 miles—Tires 4, 5, 1, 2; fifth 3,000 miles—Tires 5, 1, 2, 3.

Thus, each of the nine tires will be used no more than 12,000 miles.

THE PROBLEM OF THE MARKED FOREHEADS . .   Page 28
Alex reasoned to himself as follows: Either the cross on my forehead is blue or it is green. I see a green cross on the forehead of Tom and I see a green cross on the forehead of Joe. Each of us has his hand up because each of us sees at least one green cross. If my forehead were labeled with a blue cross, Joe would be putting his hand up solely because he sees a green cross on the forehead of Tom, while Tom would be putting his hand up solely because he sees a green cross on the forehead of Joe. But each one, seeing that my cross was a blue cross, would realize very soon that he was raising his hand because he saw a green cross on the forehead of the other. Being intelligent boys, either of them would have folded his arms by this time in the realization that his cross must have been marked green. For if the cross on Tom's forehead were blue, Tom would realize that Joe would not be raising his hand at all, and if the cross on

Joe's forehead were blue, Joe would realize that Tom would not be raising his hand at all.

Therefore it appears that both Tom and Joe are a bit confused and cannot make the foregoing deduction. The only reason that they cannot arrive at this conclusion must be that I am *not* marked with a blue cross.

THE PROBLEM OF
THE DIFFICULT
CROSSING . . . Page 29

Four trips. First he takes the duck over, leaving the dog alone with the corn. Then he takes the dog over and brings back the duck. Then he brings the corn over and leaves the corn with the dog. Then he comes back for the duck.

THE PROBLEM OF THE
FRUIT PEDDLERS . Page 30

The peddlers all had this sign on their pushcarts:

```
Apples
3 for 10¢
```

The first peddler, who had fifteen apples, sold his apples to five customers at three for a dime, thus receiving fifty cents. The second peddler sold nine of his apples to three customers at three for a dime, thus receiving thirty cents, and then sold five customers a single apple each at four cents apiece, thus receiving twenty cents, or a total of fifty cents.

The statement that a sale at four cents each is a "three-for-ten cents" rate cannot reasonably be challenged. If you are unconvinced, go to a market and attempt to buy a single item which is marked "three-for-ten" at less than four cents.

The third peddler sold three of his apples to one customer for a dime, and then made ten individual sales at four cents each. He, too, realized the sum of fifty cents.

The same result ensues if we postulate a market sign of "six-for-a-quarter." Here, of course, the individual sale of a single apple would be made at a rate of five cents apiece. The total yield under these conditions for each peddler would be sixty-five cents.

THE PROBLEM OF
THE MURDERED
WOMAN . . . . . Page 31

Answer: SPUD

Analysis

A) Dan is innocent because he couldn't be the murderer if either of his statements is true.

B) Mat is innocent for the same reason.

C) Red is innocent because if we assume that he is guilty the following statements become true:

Red: Me and Mike were together from 10 to 12 away from the rest of the gang.

Mike: I never saw a gun in my life.

Jim: All of us except Dan were in Chi when it happened.

In view of this true statement by Jim, Spud's second sentence becomes false, rendering his first one true:

Spud: Only one of us witnessed the murder.

Now since the woman's murder was witnessed, and since Red and

Mike were together at the time, Mike must have been the witness. But this leads to a contradiction in view of Mike's true statement.

D) Jim is innocent because if we assume that he is guilty the following becomes true:

Jim: All of us except Dan were in Chi when it happened.

Spud: Only one of us witnessed the murder.

Dan: I was in Philly when it happened.

Mat: I was at the neighborhood movies, at the time, with some other one of the boys.

Red: Me and Mike were together from 10 to 12 away from the rest of the gang.

These statements are contradictory because Mat's statement above can't possibly be true in view of the above facts. With whom did Mat go to the movies? Not with Red, Mike, or Dan, according to the foregoing. Obviously, it couldn't have been with the murderer, Jim. And Mat specifically excluded Spud as his companion. He said. "Spud's the murderer. I was at the neighborhood movies, at the time, with *some other one* of the boys." If this last statement is held true, then the assumption of Jim's guilt must be dropped.

E) Mike is innocent because if we assume that he is guilty then the following statements become true:

Dan: I was in Philly when it happened.

Red: Me and Mike were together from 10 to 12 away from the rest of the gang.

If Mike was the murderer and Mike and Red were alone when the woman was shot, then Red must have been the sole witness. This makes Spud's statement: "Only one of us witnessed the murder," a true statement. Spud, then, must have made a false statement when he said: "I was not even in town on the night of the killing." Of course, then, Spud *was in Chicago* on the night of the murder. So was Mat. He went to the neighborhood movies, with "some other one of the boys." With whom? His statement specifically excluded Spud as his companion; Dan was in Philly; Red and Mike were at the scene of the crime; therefore, the only one of the boys that could have been at the movies with Mat would have been Jim. This analysis places all the men in Chicago on the night of the murder, with the exception of Dan. If this is so, then Jim's statement: "All of us except Dan were in Chi when it happened" must be true, rendering Jim's first statement "Mike pulled the trigger" false.

F) Spud is the guilty man. He is so proved through a process of elimination. Although he cannot be directly proved to be guilty, no statement or fact conflicts with the theory of his guilt. Since one of the men is guilty by hypothesis, it must be he. Assuming Spud guilty, the following statements become true:

Dan: I was in Philly when it happened.

Jim: All of us except Dan were in Chi when it happened.

Spud: Only one of us witnessed the murder.

Red: Me and Mike were away from the rest of the gang when it happened.

Who was the witness? Well, either Mat or Jim. For if Spud is guilty, Mat's statement: "I was at the movies, at the time, with some other one of the boys," becomes false.

THE PROBLEM OF THE
COMMUTER . . Page 32

The chauffeur, meeting Brown at some point between the residence and the station, saves 20 minutes from his usual trip by not being obliged to proceed from the point where Brown is met to the station and then *make a return trip* to that point. In other words, the chauffeur saves the run of double the distance from the point where Brown is met, to the station. The saving, amounting to 20 minutes in all, means a saving of two 10 minute runs. Therefore, the chauffeur met Brown 10 minutes before he would usually arrive at the station. Since he usually arrived at 5 p.m., he met Brown at 4:50 p.m. Since Brown arrived at the station at 4 p.m. and was met at 4:50 p.m., he walked 50 minutes.

THE PROBLEM OF THE
JUGGLING JUGS . Page 33

First step: From the biggest jug, which now contains 8 quarts of oil, pour 5 quarts into the 5-quart jug. This leaves 3 quarts in the biggest jug.

Second step: Take the jug that has 5 quarts in it, and pour 3 quarts into the smallest jug.

Third step: Take the 3 quarts from the smallest jug and pour it into the largest jug. You now have 6 quarts in the largest jug, 2 quarts in the middle-size jug, and nothing in the smallest jug.

Fourth step: Pour the 2 quarts from the middle-size jug into the smallest jug. The middle-size jug is now empty. There are 6 quarts in the largest jug and 2 quarts in the smallest jug.

Fifth step: From the largest jug, fill the middle-size jug. The three jugs now contain the following: the largest jug has 1 quart; the middle-size jug has 5 quarts; and the smallest jug has 2 quarts.

Sixth step: Pour 1 quart from the middle-size jug into the smallest jug. That leaves 1 quart in the largest jug; 4 quarts in the middle-size jug; and 3 quarts in the smallest jug.

Seventh step: Pour the 3 quarts from the smallest jug into the largest jug. You now have 4 quarts in each of the two larger jugs.

THE PROBLEM OF THE
VANISHED COIN . Page 34

The coin which had been inadvertently mislaid was a great rarity. The stranger, being a collector of antiques and coins, happened to have in his vest pocket the only other specimen extant of the coin which Lewis had brought from the continent. If the stranger submitted to a search of his person, the prize coin would have been found upon him and he would have been accused of stealing it. If he resisted the accusation of theft, his own coin would have been taken from him, since all would have avowed that the coin belonged to Lewis. The stranger did not wish to lose his own valuable coin. The reason that the stranger did not exhibit his own coin to the assembled guests in the first instance was that since he was an invited guest it would have been a breach of propriety to steal the show from Lewis, who was a member and inordinately proud of his prize find.

THE PROBLEM OF THE
WHIFFLEBIRD . .   Page 36

Astounding as it may be, half the foliage was gone no earlier than the thirtieth or last day. Since each day twice as many leaves were eaten as on the previous day, on the thirtieth day twice as many leaves were eaten as were consumed on the twenty-ninth day.

Now the total number of leaves eaten on the thirtieth day was greater by one than the total number of leaves consumed on the first 29 days. This can be demonstrated by merely accounting for (let us say) 5 days. On the first day, 1 leaf was eaten. On the second day, 2. On the third day, 4. On the fourth day, 8; and on the fifth day, 16. The total number of leaves eaten during the first four days equalled 15 leaves, while on the fifth day the number was 16, or one more than all the others combined.

This mathematical relationship will hold true no matter how many days are reckoned. There will always be one more in the last number than there will be found in the total of all previous numbers combined.

The question is when was half the foliage consumed. If we were dealing with only 5 days, 15½ leaves would constitute half of the total of 31 leaves. But since only a total of 15 leaves would be eaten in 4 days, we would have to wait until the fifth day to account for that extra half leaf which would bring the figure up to 50%. Similarly, in the given problem, half the foliage was not consumed until the thirtieth day.

THE PROBLEM OF THE
CAT IN THE WELL .   Page 37

Thirty-one minutes. In the first two minutes, the cat climbed one foot. In 30 minutes, the cat climbed 15 feet. During the next minute, the cat would have gained the necessary three feet to reach the top. Once at the top of the well, there would be no more sliding back.

THE PROBLEM OF THE
LADY AND THE
TIGER . . . . . . Page 38

Before the waiting populace, he plunged his hand into the box, drew forth a paper, and then without reading it, plunged it into his mouth, and chewed it, and swallowed it. He then calmly announced that the king's chamberlain would read the remaining piece of paper. Whatever word was written on the remaining piece of paper in the box, the one that he, the candidate, drew forth from the box was clearly the other alternative. Since the paper that was left had the word *Tiger* on it, it was clear to everybody that the young man had indeed won the princess.

THE PROBLEM OF THE COUNTERFEIT
Two . The wise man divided the nine coins into three groups of three. First he weighed Group A against Group B. If they balanced, then he knew that each of the coins in these groups were of the same weight, and therefore each of these six coins were made of pure gold.

The counterfeit would then be found in the last group of three. He then took any two of the last three remaining coins, and put one of these two coins on each side of the scale. If these two coins balanced, then the counterfeit coin would have to be the last unweighed coin. If the two coins did not balance, then of course, the lighter coin—the one on the scale that went up—would be the counterfeit coin.

Now suppose that in the first instance, when weighing the two groups of three, one side of the scale went up. It would then be clear that the lighter coin was among this group of three. The sage would then proceed, as stated above, with the three coins among which the lightest one was to be found.

THE PROBLEM OF
The answer to Sir John's question is the color white. Restating the problem, it seems that Sir Burton walked three miles due south, then five miles due east and that he was then only three miles away from where he first started. This would be possible only under one condition—if he had started walking from the North Pole.

It is not possible to go north of the North Pole—or east or west; you can only go south. If Sir Burton started walking from the North Pole and traveled three miles due south, then no matter how far he traveled due west or east, he was no further than three miles from the North Pole.

As the only kind of bear to be found in the region of the North Pole is the Polar Bear, which is white, then on the trip in question, Sir Burton must have shot a white bear.

THE PROBLEM OF
Thirteen trains. Since it takes six hours to make the trip from Washington to New York, the train which pulls into New York as you leave Pennsylvania Station left Washington at 5 a.m. You will arrive at Washington six hours later, or at 5 p.m. You will, therefore, pass trains which left or will leave Washington at the following hours: 5 a.m.—6 a.m.—7 a.m.— 8 a.m.—9 a.m.—10 a.m.—11 a.m. —12 noon—1 p.m.—2 p.m.—3 p.m.—4 p.m. Of course, at the exact moment you pull into the Washington station, a train will be leaving for New York. If you're alert, you will also see this one. The answer then is thirteen trains. (If you count the one you're on, there'd be fourteen trains.)

THE PROBLEM OF THE
The worm traveled exactly one quarter of an inch. Standing on the

shelf, the first page of Volume One adjoined the last page of Volume Two, with only two bindings intervening.

THE PROBLEM OF THE FORTY-TWO BEERS . . . . Page 43

Who paid for the beers? Why, the American, of course! There is no disputing the fact that he paid currency each time he bought a drink. The point is that he increased the value of the currency which he got in return; that is he increased the 90¢ change he got on each transaction *by walking across the border.* He added value to the currency by transferring it from one place to another.

There is nothing more startling about this increase in value than there is about buying an object in China that is worth 10¢ there, and transporting it to America where it is worth 50¢. The American *who performed the work* of carrying a Guatelavian dollar from Tinto to Guatelavia performed 10¢ worth of work from the viewpoint of economics.

THE PROBLEM OF THE BLIND MAN . . . Page 44

The blind man reasoned thus: If there were a black hat on my head and a black hat on the head of the second speaker, then the first man addressed would have seen two black hats. He would have then drawn the inescapable conclusion that his own hat was white.

Similarly, if there were a black hat on my head and a black hat on the head of the first man addressed,

then the second speaker would have known that his own hat was white. Since neither of these men were able to draw any conclusion, it is clear that I do not wear a black hat *in combination with someone else wearing a black hat.*

The only question left then for me is: Do I *alone* wear a black hat? If I were, the second speaker would see it and would have been able to definitely conclude the color of his own hat. The second speaker would have said to himself, "My hat is not black, for if it were, the first speaker would have seen two black hats and would have known that *his* hat was white. Therefore, my hat cannot be black."

But the second speaker was not able to draw this conclusion. He could only have failed to do this because he did not see a black hat on my head. Therefore, since I and another do not wear black hats and since I do not wear a black hat all by myself, there must be a white hat on my head.

THE PROBLEM OF THE TARDY GOLFER . . Page 45

Mac figured to arrive at eight o'clock. He arrived two hours or 120 minutes later than he would have had he maintained his average speed of sixty miles per hour.

If Mac had gone along without mishap, it would have taken him one minute to traverse each mile. At fifteen miles per hour, it took him four minutes to traverse each mile. Therefore, he lost three minutes each mile traveled after the trouble started.

Since he lost two hours or 120 minutes, his car must have been in distress for the last forty miles of the trip. This means, then, that he had traveled eighty miles before his engine started to kick up a fuss.

At sixty miles per hour, it must have taken him eighty minutes to do eighty miles. Since he left at six in the morning, his car must have developed engine trouble at 7:20.

THE PROBLEM OF THE
MURDERESS . . Page 46

The answer to this perplexing problem is to be found in the fact that it is a tenet of the law in all civilized countries that the innocent may not be made to suffer with the guilty. The sisters were Siamese twins.

THE PROBLEM OF
THE DRY-GOODS
DEALER . . . Page 48

The dry-goods dealer takes the five-yard piece of material and stretches it along the edge of a piece of paper. He then adds the 36-inch width to the five-yard measurement, making a total of six yards. He folds the paper in half, which gives him a three-yard measure, and then folds this three-yard measure in half, which gives him a yard and a half measure. He then cuts the five-yard piece of material to the point indicated by the yard-and-a-half measure.

THE PROBLEM OF
THE CIGARETTE
BUTTS . . . . Page 49

Six cigarettes. Five cigarettes were made from the 25 butts. After these were smoked, there were five more butts. From these five butts, a sixth cigarette was made.

THE PROBLEM OF THE
STOLEN CAMEO . Page 50

Geoffrey Warren was considered the foremost appraiser in London. His sales were based on the reputation of his firm for both integrity and knowledge. While polishing the cameo to which he had given such unstinted praise, he discovered that it was a forgery. He had to prevent the terrible discovery from being made by anyone else. A firm like Warren and Company couldn't afford to be mistaken. They were highly reputable and were expected to know what was genuine and what was bogus. Geoffrey Warren stole the cameo to destroy it. His reputation was worth more than £50,000.

THE PROBLEM OF THE
BLIND ABBOT . . Page 52

18 monks

1	0	8
0		0
8	0	1

20 monks

4	1	4
1		1
4	1	4

24 monks

3	3	3
3		3
3	3	3

32 monks

1	7	1
7		7
1	7	1

36 monks

0	9	0
9		9
0	9	0

THE PROBLEM OF THE
HORSE TRADER . Page 53

Twenty-nine. This problem is very easy if you work it backwards. . . . The trader had one horse on which to ride home. He disposed of the next to the last horse as a trading fee when he exited from the third fair. This makes a total of two. Since he sold half of his remaining string at the fair, he must have had four in order to have had two left. He paid one to get in. So he must have arrived at the last fair with *five* horses. . . . It's a simple matter to follow through in reverse and figure out that he started business with twenty-nine.

ANAGRAMS AND
PALINDROMES . . Page 69

The letters in *new door* can be arranged to form the phrase *one word*.

THE TRACKS IN
THE SNOW . . . Page 86

The tracks were made by a peg-legged man wheeling a wheelbarrow across the prairie.

It will be observed that the single track lies between the footprint and the impression made by the butt end of a wooden stump. The two butt ends of the wheelbarrow made the two round impressions found in the middle of the picture. A wheelbarrow is wider than the width of a man across the knees, and therefore, those impressions are farther apart than the footprints. The wheelbarrow was set down when the one-legged man came to a halt. At that moment,

while resting, he brought his foot and wooden stump parallel to each other.

THE DARING YOUNG
MAN . . . . . Page 87

He juggles the balls. This way, one ball is always in mid-air, and the bridge only has to support 199 pounds at any given moment.

THE BLIND BUTLER . Page 88

Three socks.

THE ROPE LADDER . Page 89

Five rungs—for as the tide rises, the yacht will, of course, rise with it. The ladder, being attached to the yacht, will rise with the boat.

THE SCALE PUZZLE . Page 90

On Scale No. 4, we find that the pitcher is balanced by two glasses. But since, according to Scale No. 2, two plates will balance a glass, we can deduce that the weight of a pitcher is equal to the weight of four plates.

If this is so, then by removing equal weights from both sides of Scale No. 1, that is, a pitcher from the left hand side and four plates from the right hand side, we shall not disturb the balance. We are thus able to show that one glass will be balanced by two cups.

If then, we substitute on Scale No. 3 two glasses for the pitcher, we will have two glasses on the left side equalling a glass and two cups on the right side, which will leave three plates to balance six spoons.

Therefore, the weight of one plate is equal to the weight of two spoons.

Since, according to Scale No. 2, a glass is equal to two plates, and since a glass is equal to two cups, the weight of a plate is equal to the weight of a cup. We can thus remove the plate and the cup from Scale No. 5 without disturbing the weight ratio. Since a plate will be balanced by two spoons, a glass, according to Scale No. 2, should be balanced by four spoons. Consequently, two glasses will be balanced by eight spoons.

Then, all you have to do is place your hand through the loop thus formed, and then you are a free agent.

THE FARMER'S BEQUEST . . . Page 139

The figure below shows how the division is made. Note that two matches have been broken in half.

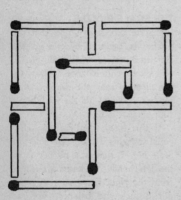

PUT YOUR HEAD THROUGH A CALLING CARD . . Page 141

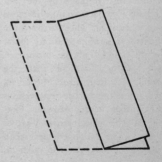

THE ROPE TRICK . . Page 140

Take your partner's rope and slip a loop of it underneath a rope tied to your own wrist.